A CLEAN BREAK

Designs and Methods That Bring Order to Your Home

By **Sandra Phillips** with **Don Aslett**

Produced by:

P.O. Box 1185
Whittier, CA 90609-1185

www.live-right.com

Book design, layout,
digital art, additional
illustrations, and production: Ryan Roghaar
www.ryanroghaar.com

Illustrations: David Lock
Cover Photography: Niel Townsend
Editor: Joel J. Campbell, M.A.

Dedication:

To all of my children, whose bedrooms
(messy and otherwise—you know who you are)
gave me excellent fodder for this book: Barratt,
Ricky, Ryan, Spencer, Nancee, JJ, Roo and
Natalee.

Acknowledgements:

JANET TOWNSEND proofread and made excellent editorial comments. She called and interviewed neighbors and children to get fresh ideas for three chapters. RYAN ROGHAAR is an extraordinarily talented artist who also did some graphics magic on the book. He is exacting in his work and unflappable by nature. JOEL CAMPBELL, M.A., edited the book from beginning to end, on a tight time frame, with finesse and confidence. BRYAN CROCKETT has worked with me on publishing several books and always does everything first class. KATHY CAMPBELL read each chapter for content and correctness, and shared stories of her own. HEATHER WRIGHT PHILLIPS shared her experiences of teaching her own daughters to work, which I included in the "Kids Clean" chapter. NIEL TOWNSEND took photographs at multiple locations to get just the right look for all of our cover work. He's a gifted young professional with an amazing artistic sense. KIM TOWNSEND did makeup magic for the cover photo shoot. CHARLENE & WAYNE WRIGHT made a huge mess on their impeccably clean staircase for the cover photo, and allowed us to film it for all posterity to see forever after. An Evening Roundtable discussion group in Hawaii gave me multiple ideas for the Spouses Cleaning Houses chapter, thanks to the brilliant thinking of TROY & NANCEE TEGEDER, SPENCER & KRISTIN PHILLIPS, and MAREK & MELISSA RAJESH. ANNE WRIGHT PHILLIPS gave me superior assistance on the Spouses chapter. NATALEE PHILLIPS and NANCEE TEGEDER were final proofreaders. REED PHILLIPS is the most helpful, neat, squared away spouse a woman could have. He came into our marriage all trained, thanks to his own mother. He helps me create a happy, peaceful home. His proofreading on the book was also invaluable.

Table of Contents

> "Clean hands, clean hearts, clean homes, clean water, clean air, clean clothes, clean minds... Clean—what a wonderful word!"
> —Richard L. Evans

Introduction: Why Clean?

Looking for the shortest, fastest, cheapest, most fun route to a stress free, organized life? It's called clean! You know the word, now you just have to switch its usage from a verb ("Clean The Room") to a noun ("Be Ye Clean"), and then we can put *it* to work instead of us.

We've labeled it a chore, a challenge, and heavily associated it with clutter and dirt—only two tiny aspects of the power of clean. But clean can infuse magic into every living aspect of life!

Clean reaches much deeper than scrubbing a visually soiled surface—it is the simplest route to an organized, stress free, happy life.

Clean is a hard sell

Clean has been (still is) a hard sell, because for centuries its use has been 90% negative.

Punishment. "You'd better behave you little… or you'll have to clean your room!"

Career. "You students better study or you'll grow up to be janitors."

Threat. "If you don't get it cleaned up, no swimming."

Humiliation. "Your mother cleans for a living? You're kidding!"

A Bride. "When you clean up the place, we'll go to a movie."

The Nag. "I've told you 100 times to clean up this…"

Prestige. "Well at least you didn't end up with a cleaning job!"

Guilt. "Live like a pig, get treated like a pig!"

Abuse. "You kids go help your mother with her cleaning."

Defense. "I don't do windows."

Scope of "Clean" the most influential virtue!
It affects...

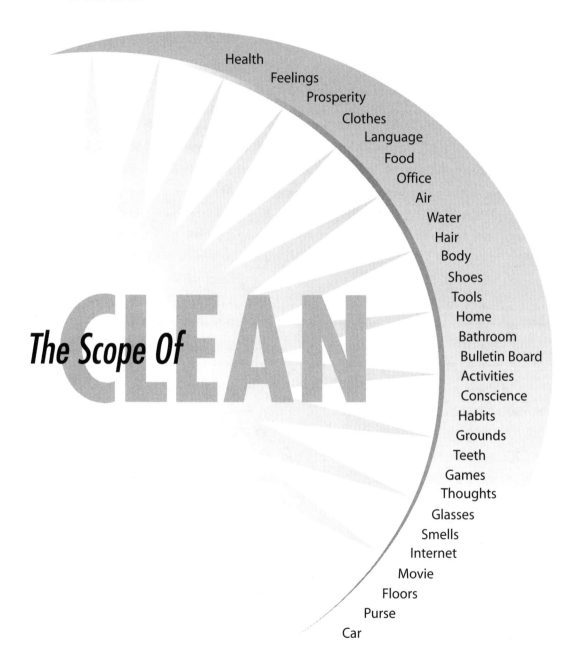

The Scope Of CLEAN

Health
Feelings
Prosperity
Clothes
Language
Food
Office
Air
Water
Hair
Body
Shoes
Tools
Home
Bathroom
Bulletin Board
Activities
Conscience
Habits
Grounds
Teeth
Games
Thoughts
Glasses
Smells
Internet
Movie
Floors
Purse
Car

If you sum it up, just about every scripture and every sermon ever preached, plus what God himself tells us—is to dejunk and clean up our life— our dwelling, clothes, body, language, cars, drawers—everything."

Doubt the power of the word CLEAN?

Wow, just imagine if each one of us was clean in heart, habit, and health. What a glorious life and world this would be!

- Police forces and policing expenses could probably be cut 85%
- Ninety percent of lawyers wouldn't be needed
- Ditto most psychologists and counselors
- Divorce would all but disappear
- There would be much less sickness and no more hospital overloads
- Life expectancy would probably go up at least ten years
- The dangerous chemicals being used in the world would be cut in half
- Pollutants in the air and water worldwide would decrease about 75%
- We'd have much less need for landfills
- We wouldn't have to rate movies, or feel uncomfortable about a movie again
- Pornography would cease to exist
- Graffiti would go away
- Certain politicians wouldn't feel a need to lie
- You could actually see a teenager's carpet
- The cost of janitorial services would be dramatically reduced
- Janitors and maids would love everybody they worked for
- There would be no need for road crews to clean up our highways
- Littering on sidewalks would cease
- No more stepping on somebody elses gum
- Fewer Dental Caries
- Bad words or thoughts wouldn't escape our lips
- Depression would be less common as visual disturbances decreased
- Everything would smell good and be fresh all the time
- There would be fewer accidents from items left laying around.
- And the best part—all the improvement would be FREE!

Pick a Feeling

Here's an interesting exercise. Read the two sides of the columns on this page — the words on the left relate to unclean, the other list of words relates to clean. Notice how you feel about each list as you read them out loud, and how easy it is to pick the side you want to live in and around, with and for...

Dirty Words	Clean Words
Grimy	Bright
Grubby	Shiny
Yucky	Gleaming
Murky	Immaculate
Moldy	Spotless
Rank	Pure
Dank	Tidy
Disgusting	Neat
Infested	Fresh
Sullied	Spruced Up
Stained	Unblemished
Blackened	Spic-and-Span
Defiled	Clean as a Whistle
Dusty	Scrubbed
Fetid	Spotless
Slimy	Dirt-free
Oily	Hygienic
Crusted	Sanitary
Befouled	Pristine
Adulterated	Polished
Putrid	Wholesome
Rotten	Clear

The Clean Guarantee

If you follow the guidelines in *A Clean Break*, we promise you the following results. You will…

- Feel better, every day and every hour
- Become better organized
- Save time
- Save money
- Have more space
- Gain self-confidence
- Increase your self-esteem
- Live safer
- Be treated better by others
- Have new freedom
- Grow spiritually
- Find peace and harmony
- Be happier than ever
- Enjoy life more
- Be treated better

Cleaning up after people reinforces bad behavior—they'll continue messing up! The commandment is "Be Ye Clean," not "Keep Them Clean." Accepting and expecting this "Clean up after me" entitlement is the foundation of a poisoned soul.

There is a stewardship involved with being entirely responsible for our conduct and condition. At home there was a Mom or a maid, at school a janitor, in sports a coach, and at camp a leader. Then we begin our adult lives, and leave all that being cared for behind. Will we live buried, behind, or on top of things? Clean isn't only a matter of soap, water, rags, and brooms, it becomes an enabler of good personal conduct and the rewards that come from it.

The goal of this brief book will be to help children, teens, and spouses understand the reward that comes from keeping our surroundings clean.

We will cover this information in four sections:

1. Conquer Housework by Designing it Out
2. Inspiring Kids to Clean
3. Teen Clean Machines
4. Spouses Cleaning Houses

Clean: A recap

If we want to live better—unaddicted, undirty, and unafraid—we need only implement to its fullest the principle of **clean**. Whenever and wherever "clean" enters our houses or habits, problems leave. Clean will solve most of our personal problems, hence most of the worlds' problems.

Clean creates harmony, peace, safety, freedom, power, and security. Clean speaks with a clear voice that all is well and in control.

The Clean Triangle

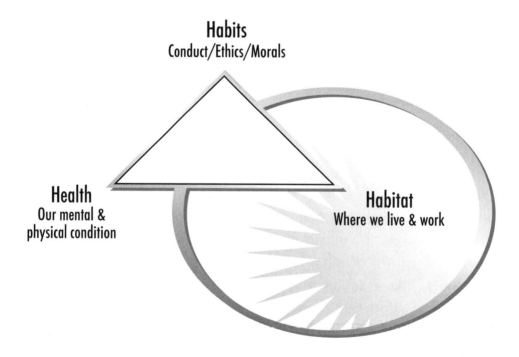

Habits
Conduct/Ethics/Morals

Health
Our mental &
physical condition

Habitat
Where we live & work

Section 1: Conquer Housework by Designing it Out

For centuries houses have been built for three basic purposes:

For shelter, for show, and for some possible economic gain through appreciation. What if we could have these things, plus a dwelling that would practically clean itself—and do more sharing than showing. This would be a home that would strengthen the family by *building in* cleaning help and efficiency. Would you be interested?

Most of us live in lazy (selfish, sluggish, slothful) homes—homes that don't work for us. We slave over them with as much intensity as we remove a festered sliver from the bottom of our foot, yet our home should be our first-line of defense and prime source for cleaning help! We've blamed ourselves for much of the disorganization when our houses should be doing the lion's share of the work. By altering their very structure and through some wise interior construction and decorative maneuvers, our homes can require less

cleaning. This concept will encourage order, keep family peace and save us time. *Our homes have been controlling us long enough.*

Don't live in more house than you need.

Cutting the square footage of our living quarters is a smart, sure way to reduce cleaning. It is completely obvious, but so overlooked. As our living circumstance changes, we may have two or three empty or unused rooms that we're cleaning, heating, insuring and paying taxes on. An oversized home can be a real handicap. As we travel around the country, we hear the same thing from people everywhere. Without exception, those who downsized after getting rid of an underused huge place said it was the most timesaving thing they ever did. They missed their old place for an average of about… sixteen minutes.

Have the courage to cut down on what you really don't need or have outgrown. If this is not an alternative at this time, at least close off your unused space. You'll save energy, cleaning, time, and avoid filling it up with trash and clutter.

A home is probably the best real estate investment you'll ever make. When the time is right, cash it in, don't let it deteriorate in value.

The best way to cut down on cleaning is to prevent it.

This is the biggest and best kept of all cleaning secrets—eliminate the need for cleaning right up front. We're talking about what you do before you ever pick up a broom, get out a bottle of cleaner, or turn on the faucet. The first principle of efficient cleaning and repair is *eliminate the need to do it at all*!

Sound idealistic? Well it's pure reality. Prevention is markedly easier than restoration, recovery or repair. Prevention saves not just time, money, and the environment, but a lot of negative stressful emotions as well. The first thing we need to do—even before picking up the perfect cleaning tool and cleaner is to reduce the causes of cleaning with some too often forgotten principles.

Camouflage where you can. Choose colors and textures in flooring, wall coverings and furniture that hide and downplay the daily dirt, droppings and spills, until you have a chance to go after them. If you want to have an orange cat, for example, it might be smart to buy an orange couch. I always tell visitors who marvel how clean my house looks, that it's totally as dirty as anybody else's—it just doesn't show. The reason? Let's start with flooring. My home has carpet that is medium gray—an exact color-coordinated match to the street dirt and air pollution in Los Angeles that filters or gets tracked in daily. My kitchen counter is a medium-colored, low satin finish that hides every crumb and grease smear the kids leave behind. My door casings aren't painted white to show every finger smudge, instead they're medium toned wood grain, stained and sealed. I don't even remember the last time I cleaned them, yet they look good enough that I'd feel comfortable hosting a wedding reception tomorrow. Even my entry floor doesn't demand immediate clean-up. It is a marbleized combo of shades of gray and soft pink. I made the grout lines very narrow, and it wipes clean with just water and a Microfiber mop. Tracked in sand or spilled food is nearly indistinguishable.

You get the idea. I don't have a lot of time to clean, so my house helps me hide the evidence until I can get to it, or until my guilt feelings overcome me. If you want to be a cleaning magician read on.

Suspend it. If you can move it off the floor or counter, by attaching it to a wall or ceiling, do so! It will take up less horizontal working or walking space, is easier to clean under, can't be drug across the surface, and won't get in your way when you're cleaning. Suspend or vertically mount small

appliances, tables, chairs, lamps, coat racks, and so on. Walls are one of the most underused parts of homes, so let's put them to work. In my home, I have all of my snack bar chairs mounted to the bar, a drinking fountain mounted to the wall and a sport climbing wall mounted to the chimney! Tissue dispensers are recessed right in the wall in bathrooms (just like hotel rooms do). I mounted a small hand dryer (instead of laying out hand towels), and a soap dispenser in another bathroom. The master bedroom television is in the wall so it doesn't have to be dusted on some table every week; yet the room remains elegant looking. Be creative! If there's a wall, there's a way.

Build it in. Built-in furniture and appliances save not only space but bumps, stubs and scratches on you and the furnishings. Tops, backs and undersides of things don't need to be dusted. You can sometimes buy readymade or contract with a cabinet maker or builder to customize your perfect built-in.

I envisioned my ideal headboard, then went shopping for it, but it wasn't to be had. A cabinetmaker took my design, which I scratched out on paper, and crafted a beautiful, built-in, functional headboard with places to store or hide books, reading glasses, tissues, earplugs and phone, security system and master lighting controls. In one area I built in an entire entertainment center complete with surrounding book cases. In other rooms are window seats, bulletin boards and carefully constructed pantry shelving for ease of cleaning and functionality.

Keep it simple. The less details and decorations, the less curves, joints, grooves, edges and ledges, the fewer kinds of materials something is made of, the easier it will be to clean and keep clean—and the less equipment and supplies you'll need to do it! A louvered or elaborately paneled door, for example, will take much longer to clean than a simple, flat door. In my home, single-handled faucets and smooth spouts are not ornate, but they are classy and easy to clean. In one of my bathrooms, I have an automatic faucet. No handles, motion activated, and simple to use. Anything with an uneven, indented, or relief-design (two offset layers) surface—from floor covering to countertop material to wall covering and doors—is going to

accumulate dirt faster and be harder to clean. Why do you think "it's the pits" got such a negative connotation?

Avoid high maintenance materials. Anything that needs constant polishing, stains easily, or shows every grain of sand or speck of lint should be avoided. For example, if you want the look of stainless steel throughout the kitchen, realize that it will never maintain an evenly polished surface—it will merely have a stained-less look. Stained less is better than stained more, however! White or light colored furniture and carpets are going to require cleaning much more often than medium and darker tones. Soft woods and highly polished surfaces will not be as forgiving of nicks and scratches. My husband and I wanted a fashionable Roman bath look in tub and shower areas without the upkeep required of polished marble. By installing a man-made material that was slightly buffed and variegated, we achieved the panache look, without the difficult upkeep. Low-maintenance materials are out there and worth seeking.

Consider life cycle costs (sustainability). Whether it's inferior quality clothes and food, or inferior quality roofing, furniture, countertops and flooring, it almost always costs more to put in a lower grade of anything in the long run—and we're all in this for the long run, aren't we? I remember the first home I built. The roofer asked if I wanted a 15-year, 25-year or 35-year roof. At age 29, I figured even 15 years would never come—so perpetually far into the future I could not fathom it. Yet, when many 60-year olds of today are asked the same question, they would probably reply, "make it the 35-year roof." It isn't just that life expectancy is so much longer—the person is more mature and envisions permanence as possible. There are objects that are purposefully transitory, like the plastic spoon or laundry detergent, but the

structure of the home should be built to last for decades, if not scores of years. By building it right the first time, 50-60% of renewable costs (for remodeling) can be saved.

Do your Housework with a Hammer. Men are generally the ones who design and build dwellings, but it's women who manage and organize the living in the home. Before I self-contracted my home near Whittier, California, I spent a year mapping out on paper just what I wanted for my family—right down to the direction of the swing on the interior doors and the vertical placement of a drinking fountain. It was a gargantuan undertaking, but I knew what I needed for eight children. Then, with rough plans in hand I began interviewing numerous architects to help bring the design to life. Some of them were annoyed by the extent of detail, and my insistence upon things like wall-hung toilets (I have six boys), central vacuum (they questioned their merit), and a shower that could work without the typical high upkeep door. Most architects were inclined to apply their typical expertise in typical fashion to create the typical house. But there was one designer who saw my vision of efficiency, though it was still in its rough stages. Steve Butcher of Chandler, Arizona, was intrigued by the assignment and took it on. Before he ever put pen to paper, I said it was vital that he read, *Make Your House do the Housework* (a book he now recommends to his own clients). It gave him an entirely new perspective of how smart design concepts could create efficiency and eliminate work inside our homes.

Don and his wife built their own low-maintenance home in his favorite spot in the world, Kauai. He did much of the construction himself on the predominantly concrete home, which uses local Koa hardwood for trim and lava rock for exterior decoration. It is in typical island style with a touch of contemporary, and looks very ordinary to the passerby, but there are dozens of subtle features which make it easier to maintain. Visit Don's website at www.aslett.com to take a virtual tour.

Each of our homes has been featured in numerous newspaper and magazine articles, and has appeared on the Discovery, CBS or HGTV television channels. We primarily used low maintenance principles that anyone can integrate. While not astonishing or magic concepts, they're just plain common sense ideas, pulled off by common people.

Now before you say, "But our house is already built" or "I can't afford to do that," consider this. Eighty percent of the high-maintenance items in our homes are things we call *roll over* items—those that we replace regularly. Paint, drapes, carpet, fixtures, flooring, appliances and furniture are some of the items in that category. Whenever you make a change or remodel you can take into account our advice, and make a few maintenance-freeing moves which will cut mega time and expense out of your upkeep schedule.

Designing from the ground up

Here are a few examples of effective structural things we and others have done in our homes to make them work harder for us—and thus reduce upkeep.

The home works *more* so that the occupants can work *less* to achieve the same end. Investigate the probability and availability of each of these applications:

Build with Steel and Concrete. Steel framing is rodent and insect proof, and nearly fireproof. Although it may be slightly susceptible to rust in humid climates if not treated, steel framed buildings are structurally exact and friendly to the environment. Currently, architectural building plans can specify just how many and what length framing member is needed, so that leftover scraps are nearly non-existent. Steel is becoming very comparable in cost to wood. Concrete can be made attractive and it's strong, enduring, soundproof, fireproof, pest resistant and childproof. Properly sealed, it gives mighty protection from the elements. Its advantage of permanence is also its weakness, in that it is not easily changed if you want to move a wall or add on. With all the new finishes and colors available, concrete is a keeper for life. Wood framed homes are traditional and an easier sell than concrete and steel; as such, the latter often loses serious consideration.

Eaves. Extend your overhangs from the typical 2-3 feet, to a generous and protective five feet. This shields a large portion of the house from direct sun and other weather damage, and eliminates the need for rain gutters. Large overhangs also reduce splash back which cuts down on the need for cleaning of exterior windows and house siding.

Roof. We built our homes with concrete roof tiles underplayed with roof felt, for an icing on the cake look that will last for a century. Roof caps are cemented on and each tile is clipped with stainless steel anchors, just in case there's an earthquake or hurricane.

Runoff control. Roofs and walks should be designed to catch and use the runoff of rain wherever possible, to water the lawns and foliage, or fill decorative pools. Some homes are even positioned to collect and recycle rainwater for toilet tanks. Consider collecting water from drains placed in parking pads and driveways. Thus runoff becomes a plus instead of a problem.

Snow patrol. No home in colder climates should be built without low voltage radiant heating. It is like capturing the sun and bringing it indoors! It warms people and objects in a home before warming room air, and it can travel in any direction unaffected by gravity. Choosing to go radiant allows you to be more comfortable at lower thermostat settings, thus saving the environment and lowering the heat bill. This natural heat transfer is both comfortable and energy efficient. Radiant heat can melt snow on sidewalks, driveways and even roofs. It can also be installed within existing walkways and structures for room heating, floor warming and snow melt. To find out more about this amazing, modern technology see www.heatizon. com.

Front doors. Don's Hawaii home has a front door that is frameless, and made of strong, decorative glass like the doors on commercial buildings. It's eight feet high, rather than the usual less than seven. If you aren't into the contemporary look of glass, you might consider what I did in my home. I have a 42"-wide oak front door. It is stained in a forgiving medium-tone and then it's carefully sealed to provide years of hard use with almost no upkeep.

Glass and window areas. Use as many windows as possible in your house, including floor-to-ceiling ones, because glass is a true low-maintenance material. It never rusts, rots, or needs to be painted. It provides exterior light for free, and if you own a squeegee, you can clean all of your windows in minutes with a few drops of dish soap dissolved in a bucket of water.

Vinyl window panes and sills. Once you have these you won't need to do any more painting in this area ever again! Vinyl windows look fresh forever and need little upkeep. Whether you are buying new or replacing windows, make sure you check into these low-maintenance wonders.

Mirrors. Mirrors used along walls of entire rooms, or mounted vertically between shelving, increase the lighting and space by double. To open up a room—consider extensive use of glass. Full length mirrors are surprisingly effective in physically protecting a wall area; they last forever, and require surprisingly minimal upkeep.

Skylights. What a great idea to open up interior bathrooms, dark attics and entries. This is a smart upgrade to take advantage of natural light and reduce electricity use. Currently, you can buy skylights which collect and focus the sun's brightness into an interior light that is shafted down from the roof line. These little lights shine bright enough to illuminate a whole room. They can't be turned off unless the sun goes down, but they have small covers which slide in place to afford day-time nappers their darkness.

Carefree ceilings. Acoustical tile absorbs sound and doesn't need painting. It's also inexpensive and easy to install and replace, so it's still a perennial favorite for many people. Painted, plastered DensGlass Sheeting is also a good product choice. It's not susceptible to mildew and moisture damage like gypsum sheetrock, and it resists nicks and gouges better. Extremely textured (stalactite-type) ceilings, especially those that are more than nine feet high, are a dust and cobweb paradise, and are hard to clean and paint. Avoid them.

Flooring. Your floor is the biggest piece of "furniture" in your home, so it needs to be right for your family and lifestyle.

Tile continues to be a favorite and will resist visible damage longer than just about any other flooring type. The ceramic type is harder on the feet and legs than other choices, tough

on toddlers learning to walk, and it's not as forgiving as carpet if you drop something. If tile is your choice, make sure the grout is medium in tone (no matter what color tile), and demand that the grout lines be very thin (1/16 of an inch instead of the usual 1/4 inch or even 3/8 inch). Your installer will moan for a few hours, but you won't need to do any of your own complaining later!

For *carpet* lovers, medium toned, variegated, dense, and low pile choices in a sculpted pattern will camouflage most spills. Always choose one shade darker than what you think will look perfect in your home. Carpet is still the most comfy to walk and play on.

Laminate flooring, including vinyl tile and sheeting, is a great substitute for natural woods that are otherwise easily damaged and not waterproof. Some companies claim that it's nearly indestructible and cannot be damaged by a falling fork or a knife attack, so check the promise in the warranty before you buy. It's a snap to keep it clean after spills, and its also easy on the legs and back for long periods of standing or pacing.

Central vacuum systems. Whether you have carpet, tile, wood or laminate, you'll want to invest in the best vacuum on the market. Instead of buying a new $100-$600 push vacuum every 2-3 years, put out a few bucks and install a central vacuum system. We've had it both ways in several houses, and speak with complete confidence that you'll love yours. The old central systems had a bad name because they didn't have motors that were powerful enough and lacked efficient connection to central sources from each room. That's all changed. By simply attaching a hose to a wall outlet, you can now vacuum anywhere, quickly and powerfully. For those who want clean, filtered air (and who doesn't?) built-in or central vacs don't redistribute dust back into the air like many conventional types.

The convenience of a built-in makes us much more likely to use the vacuum, and they work on hard or carpeted surfaces. If kids accidentally vacuum up the family hamster (heaven forbid!), conceivably they can go out into the collection tank and retrieve it (mostly) unharmed. At least we can promise that coins, rings and other small valuables get a second chance for rescue. Buy a vacuum system with the most powerful motor you can afford,

and mount it in a garage or at least in an out-of-the way closet for noise control.

Built-ins make it easy to get dirt out of corners where brooms and dust mops struggle. They pull dirt and dust down from high places without attachments, and allow you to scoot up or down steps with ease.

Decks. Decks made of concrete or concrete covered with granite or other tile are the preferred if you don't have direct sun load which heats them up to levels too scorching to walk on.

Suppliers have figured out some coatings and treatments for cement that surrounds pool areas and the like, to keep the heat dissipated—so look into those. When you get into the outdoor deck woods, even though they may be beautiful for several seasons, they require constant staining and upkeep, and tend to warp in severe heat or cold. Nails pull out, slivers surface, and spiders spin their webs.

The new composite (plastic/rubber) types are low maintenance, virtually indestructible, and will continue to look good year after year. They are treated to absorb and disperse the sun's heat, rather than hold it on the surface to burn bare feet.

Stairs. Because it's more cost effective to build "up" or "down" than buy land to spread out these days, we need to give special consideration to stairways. Make them out of cement or solid hardwood so they won't creek, sag or sway. If they are carpeted, a quick swipe of the vacuum will keep them looking nice. Avoid painted stairs and tacked on runners that bulge and crack.

Interior doors. If there is any way to eliminate an interior door, make the effort to do so. Does your walk-in closet really need that double door—or any door at all? Can the pantry be open instead of cordoned off? How about a pocket door into the bathroom, eliminating the slamming into adjacent drawer handles or walls? Keep only as many doors as are truly needed to ensure privacy. Let the rest of the house be open instead of blockaded. Doors require expensive hardware, constant adjustment, repair, and finger-spot cleaning, so reduce their numbers where you can.

Front entry. First impressions of a home are made before you ever get inside—right at the entry. Plan to cover your entry area with some type of overhang in roof design—or attach an attractive canopy after the fact. Covered entrances help prevent dirt from settling next to the house where it will be tracked in. When the entry walkway is formed, be certain that it has a 3 percent slope away from the house, so water will easily run off.

Lighting. Fixtures should be built in flush with the ceiling or walls wherever possible. This eliminates the bugs and dust that accumulate in bowl-type hanging fixtures. If it's not possible to eliminate the individual fixture, at least choose a style that will not be a collector of all flying things. For my entry chandelier, I have 40 beautiful low-voltage screw-in lights each surrounded by four small vertically hanging smoke-glass prisms. I've never had to change even one light bulb in 20 years, and the prisms only require a light annual dusting. Choose long-life, low cost, low voltage halogen bulbs wherever possible.

Fireplaces. *Wood burners* may produce heat, be romantic and deliver a festive crackling sound but they are time consuming and super messy. We love our fireplaces, but truthfully, most people use their wood burning units very seldom. The ideal wood fireplace that produces the maximum amount of heat is one that is fitted with a heat transfer grate and a set of glass doors. Such a fireplace produces more heat while the fire is burning, has a mechanism to control air flow, and reduces the amount of heat loss after the fire is out.

Gas fireplaces, on the other hand, produce safe, clean and reliable heat. They can be operated with a switch or a thermostat, right on the wall. Unlike most furnaces, many such units can be operated during a power outage. They produce less air pollution than wood heat, require very little service or cleaning, and are usually less expensive than a wood burner. Even though they lack the sound, smell and feel of a wood fire, our vote is for gas!

Storage. Design in plenty of it, right where you need it. Consider opening up unused areas in basements, attics and under stairs that were formerly walled off. Install classy shelving, including double shelves above closet hanging rods. And don't forget to assess the garage for viable space. It's normally an unused tomb

of storage possibilities. Holiday decorations can be placed in large plastic containers, labeled, and kept perfectly safe and accessible in most garages. Seasonal roasters, serving trays, fondue pots, chocolate fountains, sports equipment and unused clothes should be taken out of active space, boxed, labeled, stored, and retrieved only when needed. If you're keeping items that haven't been brought into active use for a year or more they should be sold or given away.

Countertops. These can range in price from expensive Corian® surfaces to plastic laminate. Between these two financial extremes you'll find stainless steel, plastic, granite, wood, ceramic tile and even poured concrete with pebble texture. Because most families use their counters so extensively, we offer the following guidelines:

After 20 years, my plastic laminate still looks great because it was installed well; so this is one case where most expensive is not mandatory. We are careful to use cutting boards instead of the counter, to prepare foods. There's not one burn or stain mark, just two small nicks where a knife was dropped and the point dug in. With watchful care, plastic laminate can be a good choice. If you have no budget constraints, we recommend going for a Corian-type product. Without a doubt it's the Rolls Royce of countertop options. If you burn or scratch it, you just sand it out. In any case, avoid high-shine surfaces because they show scratches more easily. Remember that muted tones are more forgiving than stark white, black or other dark colors. When you install your countertop request that the backsplash area be at least 6" high, rather than the typical 4" they will offer you. In fact, a backsplash that goes all the way up to the bottom of the cupboards is even more ideal. This saves lots of cleaning from spatters, and it looks great forever.

Cook tops. If you plan to buy a cooktop, your main choice is whether to get a gas or electrical type. *Consumer Reports* claims that many cooks prefer *gas cooktops* for stovetop cooking because they deliver immediate heat at a higher temperature, allow for instant heat control and flexibility and provide visual feedback when you raise and lower the flame. *Electric cooktops* are somewhat instant, may not quickly cool down, and

sometimes require special cookware. They are more useful for cooking at lower temperatures. My cooktop has smooth, slightly raised units that clean up easily. *Radiant ceramic* styles have coiled metal elements under tempered ceramic glass. They are fast, energy-efficient and easy to clean because of their continuous surface, with few or no food traps. The latest technology in radiant ceramic models has elements that use halogen bulbs to create high heat. These burners combine a halogen bulb with a coiled metal element. Their performance, ease of cleaning and energy efficiency are outstanding. Yes, they are more expensive. Just skip a couple nights going out to dinner and you'll have the difference in cost covered!

Faucet designs. When you begin to choose fixtures, appliances and faucets for the house, make a real effort to stick with one good brand. Replacement parts can get complicated when you have many brands. Single handled faucets are our top pick. They can be stylish and are less work to clean. Choose brushed brass or silver colors rather than high shine surfaces, so fingerprints and gunk won't show.

Avoid the ornate—really. Think of all the soap build-up that will need to be dug out of those little crevices in a few weeks. When you choose a faucet, get a little longer spout to keep splashes off the base of the handle. If you put in a new sink at the same time, pick one that is deeper than what you think you might need. This saves immeasurably on wild splashes out of the sink and will keep all kinds of spots off the mirror, making cleanup up easier.

Showers. We like walk-in, nautilus (tear-drop shape) showers, large enough that they don't require a shower door or curtain, and yet angled so that water doesn't splash out onto the floor. If this design is not feasible in the space you have, at least say, "I'm tired of shower doors" and install a beautiful curtain. They can be tossed in the washer every few months, or replaced for just a few dollars. It's an inexpensive way to update the design of the bathroom, and it saves many hours of shower door scrubbing. In any case, glass shower enclosures are suicide on maintenance.

Toilets. Between the two authors, we have eight boys, so toilet cleaning has always been a big issue. I insisted on the wall-hung type. If you know you want wall hung early on in your building process, you can anchor your toilets into steel supports, and then into the foundation for maximum strength and permanence. Mine have lasted for two decades. Wall mounted means no throat under the toilet to clean around—just as in larger public buildings like airports and many hotels. It's a cleaner, faster and more sanitary style than traditional toilets. When you ask for yours, the builder may frown— but don't give up.

Laundry Center. If you're designing your first home, consider planning the laundry room to be near the bedrooms rather than the kitchen (as is most typical). At least 95% of laundry is generated from the clothes we wear and our towels and bedding— all located in the bedroom area of the home (the other 5% is dish towels and cloths). The sounds of washing and drying can actually act as calming white noise (steady background sound) for those who are afraid that the tumble of the dryer will disturb their sleep.

We've tried it both ways, and are 100% promoters of a laundry room right next to the master bedroom if at all possible. Steps and time are saved, and it's infinitely more convenient. I also have a chute from some upstairs bedrooms that empties right into the laundry room. It's a definite plus that wasn't all that hard to work into my house plans. Convert a common wall into a space to work for you. If your own home has two or more levels, perhaps you can find a similar solution to laundry collection

Laundry. It has been determined that the most effective kitchen is "U-shaped," where traffic flows between major centers with the least number of steps. Likewise, if you have the luxury of space, or you're designing from scratch, we recommend a placement of appliances and counters in the laundry room in this order: Laundry collection, deep sink for treating, washer, dryer, folding table, stacking shelves, hanging space, ironing board, and mending area.

Kitchen. My cupboards have velvet finish flat fronts with no relief or layering of woods and laminates. This saves hours of scrubbing after dirty hands touch as they prepare yummy (but sticky) foods. Handles are smooth or non-existent for the same reason, with hinges mounted interiorly. Kitchen bar stools have no legs! They are

suspended from underneath the counter and swing in and out to allow for ease of entry and exit. That eliminates a lot of chair legs to worry about vacuuming around. Extend kitchen cabinets all the way to the ceiling to avoid the dust trap pseudo-display areas at the top. Designer plates, fake plants and plastic fruits aren't all that appetizing with cobwebs and insects sharing their high altitude homes. The high interior shelves of cupboards are perfect for storing seasonal dishes and small appliances that we don't want in active space anyway.

Furnishings and Decoration

With low-maintenance structural choices in place, next select furnishings and decorations with these qualities:

Window coverings. First of all, the perfect one is yet to be invented, although Don prefers draperies to blinds. Overall he feels that they serve the purpose of window covering at its best. Draperies need minimal dusting, and the hardware is more trouble free than in year's past. Privacy is adequate with either draperies or blinds. If it's important that you be able to control and adjust the amount of sun coming into a room at different times of the day, blinds might be a better choice. Blinds mounted between glass panes can be installed for very reasonable prices, which is just about the best of all worlds. Pay a little more here, and get the best product available, because you don't want to be plagued with mechanical breakdowns you can't get to. If you don't want or can't afford the in-the-door or window enclosed type of blind system, at least pick vertical, rather than horizontal styles, and choose vinyl for washability. They make some great styles that come in a variety of colors, or that look like wood.

Furniture. The biggest problem here is that people over-stock their home with pieces of furniture that are seldom if ever used. It's our opinion that most homes have 25% more furniture than they need. We give you complete permission NOT to line every single wall and available space with a free-standing lamp, extra coffee table, ottoman or easy chair! Give a piece away this very weekend and you'll feel like your house instantly expanded in square footage!

Choose furnishings that are simple, mutely patterned, and surfaces that are durable and washable. Sofas and chairs covered with Microfiber material keep their original color, wash up beautifully after spills, and are soft and cozy. Leather is upscale and luxurious, but probably not suitable for families with small children who have sharp toys, and shoes with buckles. If you don't have little ones to consider, leather can be a tough, durable choice that repels almost anything as long as the surface is cured. Over the years you'll see that leather holds up incomparably and becomes softer with age. Colors of all furnishings should be neutral—perhaps a little toward the darker side if there's a choice.

Strive to build in beds, drawers, entertainment centers, seating, and bookcases at every opportunity. One less thing to buy, replace, move and vacuum around or under forever after!

Walls. Don't overlook replacing a solid wall with windows to bring the out-of-doors inside. Especially in colder climates, sunshine lifts our souls! Glass is super easy to keep clean—so the more the better. Current technology also allows us to install glass that reduces heat escape and won't power up your power bill.

Neither of us is a big fan of wallpaper, but if you insist on using it buy wall coverings with subdued patterns and make sure the finish is washable. Buy a brand that promises easy removal when you tire of the pattern, or it becomes damaged.

If you know someone even minimally artistically talented and can rent an opaque projector, you might try applying a mural of a favorite scene. I had a dinosaur picture that my young boys loved. My mother captured the memory of this favorite scene by enlarging it, then inexpensively outlining and transferring the scene onto her grandson's bedroom wall. It's a classic scene that even teenagers have not wanted to remove. (Thirty years later, the new homeowners still have not painted over it.) Don has a

scene straight out of a Hawaiian village that an artist friend painted on his large curved, plaster wall. It has the effect of bringing greenery from outdoors right into his house whenever you're in the room. At least the effect confuses burglars!

Faux painting, suede finish, sponging, ragging and stippling are some popular approaches to wall painting! These techniques make for low-maintenance wall care because they don't show every little mark or smudge. They have a textured look but are much easier to clean than textured finishes. These kinds of wall paints also put a nice acrylic surface on the

wall which washes well and protects the surface. They can be a lot of fun to apply.

If you have favorite display items that you've created, received as gifts or bought on trips, find places to suspend them from the ceiling, or mount them on shelving. Every object you can get up off the floor, is one less thing to move back and forth during the cleaning and vacuuming process.

Avoid the fake and dead. Sounds gross, but many homes are repositories of bedraggled plastic flowers left over from the neighbor's last garage sale, or oversized fake copies of paintings in scratched frames that remain only slightly mitered at the corners. Then there's the stuffed animals—dozens of them—some shot (trophy type), and others bought (at county fair). Cultivate real greenery and gardens with scents in every room if possible. Corral the animals into nets and vertical hanging devices—or give them away. If you kill every plant you touch, upgrade from plastic to a better quality silk variety for a realistic look. They are washable and hold up fairly well.

Family Hub (or Control Center). Whether it's a big cork bulletin board, an oversized calendar, a whiteboard, picture board, or chalk board, there ought to be some common vertical place that coalesces the family's activities and features their accomplishments. Message and note centers, incoming and outgoing reminders, appointment cards and mail can be skillfully displayed. It becomes a living history exhibit every bit as much as a museum, and it will become one of the most popular spots in your home. Keep it well lit so friends as well as family can easily see the new Johnny VanGough that is on exhibit one week, or family vacation photos another. Kids can look at recent announcements, see notes from dad and pull down their own telephone messages all at a hub that is the nucleus of family communication.

A well-placed and well used hub saves mess, stress and emotion.

Make A Plan

These are just a smattering of proven possibilites to make your home work for you. Examine your surroundings, right now, today! Brainstorm with each member of the family and visit really efficient

commercial buildings and beautiful offices. Put your best ideas together.

To buy or not to buy. As you make your plan for purchases, consider the following:

- Will this item help the family to function better?
- How hard or easy will it be to clean? Any special equipment needed?
- How long will it stay clean and attractive in appearance?
- Does it need to be serviced, maintained or repaired regularly?
- How will you feel about caring for and cleaning it?
- How will it look down the road?

No product or idea is too crazy if it helps your family stay maintenance-free.

Free Advice. If you're still a little unsure of yourself, here's two morsels of advice from those of us who have built low-maintenance, and wish we'd done it even sooner:

1. **Don't cave in.** In life and in building there are some time-tested choices and methods that we agree are smart to follow. Some standardization is wise—being conventional can make real sense and we shouldn't burden ourselves with reinventing the wheel. On the other hand, we are all different, and adding and adjusting optional and discretionary things to suit our own unique lifestyle is exactly what we should do. Don't let the builder, architect, city engineer or inspector talk you out of what you want. Whether it's to create a sport climbing wall on the outside of your fireplace chimney, install a drinking fountain in the kitchen, or mount a wall hung toilet in the bathroom, push for your dreams. Every change

you make will benefit you over and over. And don't underestimate the impact of altering even one tiny thing—like the swing of a door in the bath room. Your family member will use it over and over, and it will help you all function more efficiently.

2. **Martha Stewart mania.** Media pressure makes us think we should pattern the physical structure and the furnishings of our homes after someone else's. New York design gurus and Hollywood house magazines tell us what is in for the season. First it's vintage, then it's contemporary, followed by "Retro"—all geared to make us feel wanting. We are hopeful that a yet-to-be-discovered illusive style will inspire our children to be more organized, get better grades; or maybe our family members will be more patient, stop swearing or lose weight. All of the answers seem to be out there, just beyond us. Because we are ever hopeful that the right colors or styles will solve our problems, we are enticed to buy

more and find our fit within the rest of mainstream America.

But it is *your* house that *your* family will pay for and live in—not a copycat Better Homes & Gardens cover page. Instead of buying more, sometimes eliminating is the answer. Get rid of extra knick-knacks from tables and all of the unused Home Shopping network devices that are building up on counters. Remove that piece of unused furniture we talked about earlier. If a home is over decorated it takes a huge amount of extra time and trouble to maintain.

For example, my husband had a business meeting in South Africa, so we took in a picture safari. On an early morning walk, we came upon an unsuspecting herd of elephants. When the largest in the group started running toward us, we had to flee for our lives down a 15-foot embankment into a nearby stream bed. Because we got this all on video camera, no one questioned our story. Once back home, we showed the video to our friends and family with great delight, but what followed after that was not a pretty scene. We began getting small elephant statues for holiday gifts, birthday and even Mother's Day. They came in wood, marble, plastic, glass and brass—by the dozens! At first I was flattered; then the elephants *took over* an entry table, a display shelf, a dining table… it was a stampede. One day I decided I hated elephants and never wanted to dust under another figurine again. So I scooped them out of my life and into an emotional withdrawal box, where they remain entombed today.

Don't start a collection unless you love the thing more than the time it will rob you of to clean and care for it. Likewise, don't be pressured into buying or doing what appears most popular, inexpensive or expedient for your home. To make it work for you, make it right for you.

Even with the structure of the house and internal furnishings working optimally, there may still be more battlegrounds. Fix these and you will save hours of upkeep.

Catch and fix down-the-road problems! Why do we put up with things around the house that don't work, let alone people and habits that

are bad for us? Sometimes we let something go on and on—for months or years! Yes, we may be too busy and tight on money to fix or change them—but we do seem to manage enough time for our favorite TV show, and we are able to scrounge up enough money to eat out, or even gamble for a weekend in Vegas.

It's more about what our commitment to personal order and household function is. Although TV soaps, beloved sports, weekend friends and fast food may be more pleasurable diversions, household annoyances can build up and aggravate our senses to the point that we can't enjoy those other things.

Top household upkeep issues

To conquer cleaning, most of us need to deal with these time wasters at some point.

Drawers and doors that stick. Forcing any door, window or drawer that isn't sliding, closing or opening easily will often cause damage. When something is operating stubbornly or not working at all, our inclination is to put more weight into it. Find the reason it isn't working and fix it, or get someone else to fix it.

Faulty, broken or missing things. A missing rubber bumper on a vacuum can bruise every door casing and baseboard in the entire house. Furniture with casters missing, faulty lamps, and flickering lights mean that trouble is ahead. Broken or half-working appliances (like toilets and showerheads!) are a daily annoyance and need to be fixed or replaced.

Plugged or slow-draining pipes. Overflows can really wreck a room, and they are a mess to deal with. You should own a toilet plunger and keep it as handy as a fire extinguisher. Set rules for what is flushed down the toilet or put down the disposal. Many people worry about the clogging of toilet paper, but it is designed to disintegrate, and is rarely the culprit for blockage.

Food control. Food has great mess potential so declaring certain parts of the house off limits for eating and drinking can really reduce our cleaning hours. Clean up spills promptly before they have a chance to become stains. Food left

anywhere compounds hourly into one of the biggest cleaning time-takers in the house.

Smoking. Cigarettes, cigars and pipes not only inflict permanent odors, they deposit a yellow-brown film on ceilings, walls, windows, and furniture. Where there is smoking there are always stray ashes and burns. The obvious way to remedy all this is to limit smoking to certain areas, or not allow it in the house at all.

Junk and Clutter. Having too much of anything is bad for homes and the people who live in them. When there is too much stuff in a space it has to be stacked up, crammed in, shuffled

Mess?
What mess?

around and leaned against things—all of which will deteriorate a room fast. As things are pulled into use from their crammed quarters, you'll find them arriving broken, torn, and wrinkled.

Hanging out. When we hang or set something on a thing or place not made for it (such as coats on curtain rods, lamps, knobs, doors or furniture), it is likely to cause warping, bending, sagging and other problems. Then we have to pay for a repair, and find another place to hang the object anyway. So put those clothes right in the closet when you bring them back from the dry cleaners. Hang the wet towel back on the bathroom rod, and don't even think about installing heavy pictures, mirrors or shelving into plain sheet rock walls without proper bracing.

Overflow. Anything with moisture in it—from flowerpots to fish tanks—should always have provision made for leaks, drips or overflow. Uncontained moisture means ring marks, rust, mildew and other damage. We've had a hot water hose to the washing machine break, and a water heater overflow several times. Fortunately well-placed floor drains can carry away much of a water disaster.

Windows left open. Open windows are wonderful for bringing in sunshine and fresh air, but you need to keep a close eye on the weather. Wind and rain will first destroy the draperies, then damage the window sills, flooring and wallboard all around.

Carpet capers. We don't usually wear out carpet from walking on it. The greatest amount of damage comes from not vacuuming regularly. This causes dirt and grit to accumulate at the base of the fibers and grind them away, resulting in compression of the pile. Good mats at entrances can also keep dirt at bay. Pet dishes and training areas should be limited to hard flooring areas. Never allow red punches to be carried (and spilled) over carpet—that's an absolute rule in our home! Those stains just don't come out. Keep drapes and curtains closed when people aren't using a room to reduce sun fade. Have a professional cleaner shampoo your carpet if you don't have good equipment or don't really know what you're doing. Even then, we suggest an extra rinse and extraction to remove every last bit of soap residue.

Train your family to avoid mess-making habits

The last way to prevent housework is probably the cheapest, and best—but it may not be the easiest to implement.

A simple change in behavior can outperform the greatest tools and techniques, or any other cleaning magic. Breaking a few mess-making actions will ease the home improvement routine, even without any structural, design or furnishing changes.

1. We can save a big chunk of cleaning and household care time if we just *put things back* right after we use them: screw lids back on, close drawers, doors, and windows. If the gate is left open, the prize family pet escapes and stray life forms may enter. Lids left off mean spilled shampoo or catsup later. Doors left open invite flies, moths and mice to enter. Windows left open are invitations for mosquitoes and birds to come exploring. Cupboard doors left open make us hit our heads; toys

and shoes left out of place cause stubbed, and broken toes.

It takes exactly the same amount of time to put a cap back on now as later, except that "later" the cap will have rolled down the drain, or onto the floor, and the abandoned tube of toothpaste will have oozed out onto the counter.

2. Don't carry dripping things across the floor or carpet. If it's wet and you must move it somewhere, put a carrier or cloth underneath. Even rinsing off hands at the kitchen sink, then dripping around looking for a towel to dry them with, puts just enough water on the floor to pull dirt off of shoe bottoms and leave mucky footprint messes behind.

3. As we disrobe, it takes the same 60-second minute to put our discarded still-clean outer clothing on a hanger whether it's now or later. Except when it's later, you have the added motion of having to stoop over and pick it up, and the clothes are probably now wrinkled. Dirty clothes will eventually have to go into the laundry basket but

it's a 2-step process instead of one single motion when we postpone the inevitable. When something is already in hand we can put it in its rightful place much more quickly and efficiently than if we toss it somewhere and have to later pick it up again. Picking up after yourself is the single most timesaving thing you can do. Don't put anything down on the nearest horizontal surface or let gravity be its master—put it away in its home.

4. Never leave anything (groceries, trash, CD's, coolers, sports equipment, etc.) in your car after use. When you get out, it gets out. We live in our cars for hours each day. They are compact and designed amazingly efficient for such a small space. There's no room or place for extras of anything except people, so any mess will accumulate at exponential speed right around our feet. Small trash bags should be placed in both the front and rear areas of the vehicle, and kids should not be allowed to leave the car until every loose item and bit of garbage is picked up.

5. The fridge is probably second only to the family car in our lineup of abused interior spaces. Each week, one person should be assigned to move older foods to the front of each shelf so they can be used, or discarded. Wipe the bottom of sticky jars (like pickles) after use, before putting them back away. Packages of meat and poultry that have just been removed from grocery bags or the freezer and set on the refrigerator shelves are likely to leak juices over everything else below. Immediately put these foods in a leak proof container or into a lined meat keeper drawer.

6. Leaving shoes wherever you pull or kick them off is plain bad. People trip over them and they look unsightly. Buy and wear shoes that don't have black heels or soles so that hard flooring doesn't get marked up. If you are coming in from outside, particularly if you've trekked across grassy areas, check the bottom of your shoes for dog doo-doo and mud. Many families even have a no-shoes policy in the house. If this is your choice, install

attractive shelving by the entrance where everyone can *place* their shoes, not just *pile* them.

Much of the mess-making we do each day may not be with malicious intent at all, but simply a matter of not paying attention to what we are doing. We saunter into the family room (and plop down in a chair), have a pop (then set the empty can down on the nearest surface), read a paper (leave it unfolded all over), take off our shoes (but one sneaks under the edge of the chair), open a magazine (when a blow-in enclosure escapes), unwrap a piece of candy (and the wrapper falls in our lap), peel an orange (and the essence sprays onto furniture like an atomizer), and so on. We can save ourselves a world of work by simply becoming more conscious of what we do and by helping other family members do the same. If no one ever acknowledges that a problem exists, resentment builds up, not contentment.

The physical structure of the home can be a tool to strengthen any family.

Summary. We've given you a glimpse of the proven possibilities of making a Clean Break through structural and furnishing details as well as some mess making problems to avoid.

House planning or remodeling plays a huge part in giving you more time with less stress around the home. Some estimate that it will save 40% of your home care time and expenses. Even if you apply just one principle you've learned in this chapter, you will forever save wasted minutes and all the stress in that one area. The more principles you apply, the more your family will benefit.

We need to take whatever steps are necessary "to make the places [we] spend time in as inspiring, beautiful and liberating for your spirit as possible" (Elaine St. James). Instead of grooming a house that merely functions for just shelter and show, we can, by careful planning, create a home that shares—not only with neighbors and friends, but with our own families. It shares opportunities to glean and clean, to work and succeed, to perform and be praised, to help organize and nourish.

Section 2: Inspiring Kids To Clean

When do our kids finally transition into that self-sustaining adult age where they are responsible for their own behaviors? That's the big question for most of us who are raising children or grandchildren! The World Health Organization studied the different ages that children from various countries became functional adults. Researchers determined that most kids from technologically advanced countries outside the United States reached adulthood between 16-17 years of age. In the United States, however, we are still coddling our kids well into their early twenties!

So perhaps we need to begin some serious, more focused parenting efforts much earlier than we currently do. A professor once said, "Students come into my office looking for a place to plug in their umbilical cords. Parents fail to teach their children how to get along in the world…young people have to learn self-discipline [after] they leave home."

Some of us spend more time planning a two-week vacation, buying just the right gifts for Christmas, or getting the car detailed than training our child to organize his room, clean a toilet or cook a meal.

And the job list we so carefully put together that one month when we were really pumped up on perfect parenting? To our kids it was no different than hanging a "most wanted" sign at the post office! They looked at it, shrugged, shook their head, even cringed—but they supposed it wasn't really their problem—so they walked away.

At least half of our parental frustration from earlier years of failed job lists was probably our own fault because we simply didn't follow through enough times. Or maybe we didn't take the time to train our kids by working alongside them. Perhaps we showed minimal interest in the whole homemaking process ourselves and we got a job out of the kids that reflected the same. Some of us thought our kids weren't ready for tasks. The reasons are many.

Why don't kids do as many household jobs nowadays?

- Parents have condos and apartments where yard maintenance is provided
- Parents use money to buy convenience products that make scratch cooking next to non-existent
- Parents remember how much they hated chores when younger and want to spare their kids
- Parents tend to be more lenient and less authoritarian
- Parents don't expect immediate obedience—they negotiate with kids
- Parents want their kids to be friends more than children
- Parents feel work may traumatize kids
- Parents are affluent and buy cleaning services
- Parents are gone long hours so they don't want to waste what few hours they have together fighting with the kids to clean when they could be "having fun" as a family
- Parents get fatigued using lists, charts, files, cards, wheels to set up jobs.
- Parents don't follow through and are not consistent with children on their jobs.
- Parents don't make time to train kids by working alongside them
- Kids are over-scheduled. There's barely enough hours for homework, lessons, practices and dinner
- Kids try to put parents on guilt trips
- Kids claim they can't do the task at hand—it's too hard
- Kids are too busy with their own friends and on the computer
- Kids friends don't have to do the work, so why should they?
- Kids have many distractions which make them focus on other things
- Kids think they do more than their own share already
- Kids say parents don't like the way they do things anyway
- Kids don't like the kinds of jobs they get assigned

When you think about it, household care and cleaning is one of the few ways parents have left to bond with and teach their children necessary delayed gratification skills. They do a job—they get rewards: praise, a cleaner room, more confidence and control, and a good feeling. A tidy house can be a sideline advantage compared to what the child gains from the cleaning experience.

Strategy & logic of cleaning. The psychology of it all! Children need to make the connection that our homes are something more real than just a load of 2 x 4's nailed together with some shingles slapped on top. We want our homes to be places where we really live, not just a glorified bed/breakfast stop. The home is something which lives to serve and grow the family. Tell children to think of the home as our larger body. "If we get sticky fingers from eating, we wash them off and it feels better; if we step in the mud, we can change out of our soggy shoes; when our play clothes get sweaty and dirty we dump them in the washing machine. Likewise, our house needs to have a bath and get cleaned up sometimes. It doesn't like having a dirty floor, smudgy windows or a ring around its toilets. We have to help it get clean, just like us!"

A healthy home is a clean home, and if we can keep it clean we'll all feel better. Tell children, "If germs are whisked away, we'll get fewer colds. When we vacuum, and dust we have fewer allergies. If we clean corners and cobwebs, we'll see fewer bugs," and so forth. Take a digital picture of a clean room, and post it so the child will know the standard of clean that is acceptable in your house. It's simply embedded in a mother's genes that clean is good, and dirty is bad but this concept must be gradually transferred to our children.

> When our home is in order, friends like coming over. "They want to play at our house when books, games, adventure toys and dolls are in their own buckets, bags or on shelves. Friends don't like to dig through messes. They would rather go to somebody else's house!

Some effective kid-approaches to improve the cleaning mind-set.

We have learned that adults generally can do needed tasks on demand, but most kids need some type of schedule, extra incentive or motivation. So let's talk about a few:

Pretend you are going to rent your house out to visitors for the week. We actually did this! A few years ago, Dave & Jodi Young and their wonderful family from Salt Lake City, Utah, traded houses with our La Habra Heights, California house for a week. As we worked to get our home looking its best for our visitors (who would be intimately acquainted with every closet and cupboard…), we made it a contest. Five of our kids—elementary through high school age—got energized as they worked to create the perfect "model home rooms" (this would also work if you "pretend" sell your home, or go on a vacation). I asked the kids how they would want their bedroom, bathroom and play areas to look to the people who will live in them. As unfair as it may seem, first impressions do matter in life, so children might as

well learn that lesson right out of the chute. The kids all slaved like over-paid custodians to get things ready. In the end, detectives could have brushed our home for fingerprints and found none. It was all a fun challenge!

Use the magic of now. Sometimes less is more. Seems strange, but the less we clean our houses, the more work it takes when we finally do. Keeping up on daily or weekly tasks like cleaning the sinks, toilets, emptying magazines and trash, is an investment in less time spent on cleaning later. As we work with kids on their various cleaning projects, a few well-timed remarks like "Wow! If we'd emptied this old yogurt out of your garbage can last month, you wouldn't have to clean out the whole can today," or "If you do a light feather dusting on your shelves each week, you'll be able to skip the bigger job of removing all your things from the shelf, dusting, and replacing them each month" and so forth. On this subject, be alert not to get things so nice/upscale for kids rooms, that they become complicated to clean. You may encourage them to personalize their room with trinkets, whatnots, McDonald's toys and blue troll dolls all over the place, but when these things become a burden of care and cleaning time, it will suck life out of you and your child.

Get some attitude. Most of the definitions of "work" are actually very positive. Synonyms such as act, do, perform, bring about, succeed, happen, design, create, produce, handiwork, run, and operate are pretty lofty. Only three definitions—labor, drudgery, and toil—are more on the negative side of the word "work," yet, most of us grow up thinking work is bad. A "let's get this done so we can finally play and have some fun" attitude needs to shift. Cleaning itself has to be fun!

With careful thought, housework can be portrayed as a positive. In a recent survey of several hundred kids, 97% of them actually "felt they should help." Although there's some training involved, it will give them and us an immediate payback unlike most other investments of time. Plus, think about it…there are few things kids can do today that give them a greater sense of completion than housecleaning! The best way to handle a messy room is not to shut the door but to open our mind and our attitude. Room

management will lead your child to self management, which later leads to home management and onto life management. And let's not get confused—remember, they are cleaning their rooms for them, not for us!

Someone said, "If you make it fun, it will get the job done."

As parents feel about and treat the house, so will the kids! If we are proud of the house as our family's home, no matter its size or age, we must not complain about how grungy it is. The kids may then reason, "If our house is such a dump, why bother to clean it up or keep it clean?" Moreover, nagging our spouse for a needed paint job, a new door, floor, or even a new home, sends a strong message that what we have isn't worth keeping. There's nothing wrong with planning for some home improvements, but watch your attitude about your existing structure. Kids mirror most everything.

Each time we clean the house as a family, or as parents, we ought to glorify in the experience. Even if it's forced in the beginning, put a smile on your face and dig in. Put on the music, and whistle. One of my favorite family songs was a little piece about cooking carrot stew together—"it's our favorite thing to do!" the lyrics said. It was spunky and made us all work faster and happier. We laughed and worked and loved doing it. Families must have a "We are proud of our home and it's working for us!" attitude. "We keep our home clean because we care about it."

Parental obligation. Most kids don't really care what their bedrooms look like; clean or dirty, tidy or chaotic, it's no big deal either way. They don't care a lot about the whole rest of the house either. Perhaps the entire neatness hysteria is completely adult-imposed, but something in our instinctive parental natures tells us that we should be teaching our offspring discipline, order and cleanliness. Studies back us up, of course. They say that visual disturbance (clutter) from chronic disorganization is a breeding ground for depression—to say nothing of things getting broken, lost and dirty.

It seems most new parents make fun interactive games out of putting puzzle pieces and shaped cubes back in their places when kids are tots, but then something happens. Right when we really need them to begin picking up their stuffed animals, or putting their dirty clothes and towels in the laundry hamper (same brain process as doing a baby puzzle), we start calling it house<u>work</u>! Because "Dad and Mom must go away to work," or we are told to "Work before you play," and we say, "No friends until the work is done," work becomes a negative about the same time the kid is toilet trained.

We sure won't get a vote anytime soon from the kids to spruce up the house though. Their excuses are all over the place and well practiced. While they may not care that their room looks lived in, eventually they need to learn that their clothes need to look something other than slept in—just as people won't be impressed with teeth that look like they've just eaten a cob of corn and a pint of blueberries. Any cleaning job may seem futile, but they are necessary. Who's ever heard of a no-wash dish or a no-wax floor? It may be a repetitive action, but it's part of learning personal discipline.

In every household that has a school-aged life form in it, there's going to be science papers due tomorrow, birthday parties, puppies born, trips to the emergency room, church talks to prepare, unexpected visitors, church shoes to buy, PTA cookies to bake and family trips to prepare for—times 50!

In the midst of all this living, there are several important reasons for teaching kids to keep their surroundings clean and orderly 1) to learn some personal regulation that we hope will carry over into adulthood, and 2) to help create family unity, as we'll explain later, 3) to gain some self respect and 4) to feel more in control of their surroundings, instead of the surroundings controlling them.

Just like adults put off writing in journals, paying bills, losing the weight, inviting friends over or jotting the required thank you note, we also

wait for the "less busy" day to teach our young child how to work. We will always be too busy to have the time to teach homecare skills—unless, of course, we make it as much a priority as getting the same kids ready for school each day, or doing our regular grocery shopping or brushing our teeth.

The first thing we need to do is bump the whole training process up a notch in worth and importance. Just as the benefits of good food ultimately produce a healthy body, the benefit of working alongside the child—teaching consistency and preparation for delayed gratification— cultivates a more contented, directed child. Pam Young (Parade Magazine 1/22/06) said, "The need to organize is more intense now with multi-tasking parents and busy kids."

Work with the kids: Team and Shadow. Even though you may see early indicators that your child is one who wants to avoid jobs and would rather play, his ability to stay on task can be improved—and surprisingly, it isn't best done through lectures or punishments. As we work with (not send) our children and they learn to focus their attention on a job at hand, you will see that their ability to exercise control over themselves in all areas increases dramatically.

In a survey of several hundred kids, 97% felt they should help around the house. Perhaps deep down, most kids sense a natural "keep the cave clean" mentality that's a carryover from primal days. It's certainly a given that parents want kids to share in the housework. We just need to figure out how to make it fun and appealing for them.

How do we get the kids to buy in? We do shadowing. It's the best way to guarantee consistent, continuous help from the children. By moving alongside children, and guiding the work process without eclipsing their responsibility or overtaking their actions, we help them master the art of self-control. Shadowing will consistently produce beds that get made, clothes that get hung, books that get re-shelved and toilets that get flushed. Use wisdom here to not overshadow (doing it for them or demanding perfection).

Team approach. One of the most effective family efforts toward keeping the house clean that I've used, is to have an evening "pick-up" time. Kids are resistant to go to bed anyway, and excited to stay up a bit later, for almost any reason—even cleaning. Each family member, including mom and dad, picks up "x" number of things in a designated period of time. Set to music that becomes recognizable (just like a gong or bell going off), you can pick up things around house by numbers of items (one item for each year of age), letters of the alphabet (anything a-m, or m-z), color (all darks or lights), size (larger or smaller than a baseball mitt) or by room. This ritual becomes a routine that's expected and accepted by the family. One of my daughters-in-law reports that her 4-year old loves to clean alongside her at the end of the day because "we play like we are cleaning a castle and she is Cinderella…we role play while we clean." What a great idea for little girls! Maybe boys would like to be worker robots, Transformers, or Bob the Builder! All little kids live in a fantasy world. They like magic and fairytale thinking which links them to reality. Let them pretend to be secret elves or Tinkerbell or little brownies, and do surprise jobs for their siblings. Put cloth puppets on their hands, so the puppet can clean up the blocks or dust the table legs. Teach your child how to use a soft dustpan to scoop up small toys and blocks and make that job go faster. After you return from the store, make a human chain putting away groceries. This makes things go faster and everyone feels involved and needed.

A UC California at Riverside study of more than 3,500 children and their parents found that "…school-age children who do chores alongside their fathers have more friends, are happier and behave better in school."

Doing all of this fun work together makes children feel like they are integral to the family; at the same time it will give you precious chances to chat and banter with them. "Sometimes the best conversations happen while you're focusing on something else, such as washing dishes or folding laundry." ("Spend time with children" pamphlet from The Parent Institute)

Usually families plan an outing, or an escape to reward themselves, or to assure balance and happiness. How about staying at home for a change, and working together on a massive project in the attic, basement, garage, junk closet, or even the child's own room?

It can have the same salubrious effect. The act of family-centered cleaning can create a new, healthy familial bond while learning or mastering cleaning skills. Can't cleaning or organizing a big project count as a stimulating adventure? When families work together on household cleaning and organizing projects (even remodeling) there can be age appropriate components in the most seemingly complex tasks—and yes, it will be remembered as an adventure.

Occasionally make a list of jobs that need doing and an estimate of the time required. Furnish a bell to be rung as each job is completed—starting with the youngest child. When her job is done, she rings the bell. She and the bell then move onto the next sib, whom she helps until his job is done. Bell rings and onto the next older child, then parent No. 1 and No. 2 until everyone is helping each other.

When we were building our family home in California, each evening I would gather up the children, ages 4 to 16, and head into the hills to remove all the construction mess that had accumulated that day. We all used caution to wear gloves and not work in dangerous areas, but each child had something age appropriate that they could pick up, scrape up, wipe down, clean off, or gather up. Most trash was deposited in an oversized on-site dumpster. Another child swept the concrete floor until everything shined by dark. Each sub-contractor commented that they'd never worked on a cleaner construction site. Years later, each child feels a genuine ownership in the home because they worked on it! Much more than a house was built thar year!

If you need some team support beyond your own family activities, hook up with Community programs and helpers. Involve children in 4-H, YMCA camps and Boy and Girl Scouts of America, etc. Youth programs with peers that teach life skills through activity and merit badges, and high adventure are invaluable for our children. One of my daughters was in the Girl Scout program for a time and my six sons became Eagle scouts. Some of the best merit badges (there's 120 to choose from!) in the BSA program that specifically teach our younger teens to gain career and interpersonal skills are Citizenship in the Community, Cooking, Family Life, First Aid, Gardening, Home Repairs, and Personal Management. Haven't we all noticed how a child will listen, behave, and follow an outsider far better than they will their parents? So, use them! Any help is good help.

Lavish Praise. Children get motivated from the inside, and from the outside. Giving verbal approval about the job they have done is a huge reinforcer from the outside, of good feelings about themselves. As soon as they gain confidence from completed tasks, their motivation will shift, and come more and more from within—requiring less demonstrative approval.

After each job is successfully completed, assure your son that his work ethic pleases you—which will be reward enough if you start early. A successful cleaning experience makes him feel better about himself and his surroundings because of what he does and what he contributes. As the child gets feedback that he's doing well, you will find that he starts being more responsible in other areas as well.

I have a daughter who was just about ready to quit her new part-time catering job. Not because of the long hours, sore feet and demanding nature of the job—she was expecting and ready for all those things. After her initial hiring, she showed up at each job, with dozens of other servers, not knowing who to report to. Everyone just started unloading the serving truck and pitching in as seemed logical. No training was provided, but most important—no feedback at the end of each job about how she was doing. Just when she was about ready to throw in the terry serving towel, a colleague emerged and identified herself as one of the owners. She had been watching the new hire and was impressed with her work ethic and invited her to serve at some special private jobs. At last, some acknowledgement! It was just a few words of approval, but enough to let her know that she was needed and appreciated. All of us need support and praise, and parents must be the first source of providing it abundantly for our children.

Some parents choose to give monetary rewards to acknowledge their children's household work.

There are two prevailing thoughts on allowances:

The anti allowance parents: No kid should be paid for helping out around the house; it's just their responsibility. Giving kids pay gives them the mistaken idea that there's a choice to skip chores when they don't need money—even though the chores need doing.

The pro allowance parents: They want to give tangible rewards for efforts and believe it motivates kids to do extra jobs around the house. Reward doesn't always need to be in the form of money.

However you decide, remember that very young children seem inclined to either save every coin (won't share a penny), spend every coin (down to the last penny) or share every coin (give away every penny). Since none of these are terrific options, we suggest that parents opt to wait until the child has a "sense of the cents"—probably around school age.

Additionally, we should never give our children the idea that we can control their actions with money, because that leaves them feeling powerless. Money must be a separate issue from job responsibility, right from the beginning. Eventually they do need some of their own money so they can learn to be good stewards and manage it well. They will learn that cheap toys fall apart faster and when something costs more, it must be purchased after saving up awhile. Ultimately, allowances should be matched to age, the family's income, and what the money is meant to cover.

One family seals into separate envelopes a prize such as trip to the park, ice cream after dinner, bubble bath, visit grandma, movie, supper out, etc, which acts as an incentive for doing the big project. It's opened after all the Saturday work is done.

> My son, J.J. was barely old enough to read some of the road signs along a long stretch of freeway. When he saw the "Litter Removal next 5 miles" sign, he asked his dad, "Is this where we can dump our garbage out of the car?"

Don has a fun "grandpa" incentive tradition that he used to instill work ethic with his grandchildren when they were young. Sometimes planned, other times unannounced, he does bedroom inspections. Without chastising or making fun, he examines around and under the bed, closets and books on shelves. Is the dirty clothes hamper overflowing? Is the floor covered with toys or CDs? How recently has the trash been emptied? He doesn't insult, he teaches; and he never uses sarcasm. Depending on how good of a job they've done, he leaves a greenback on their bed. This is another method of showing praise and approval. We feel Grandparents have the prerogative to bestow treasures on their grandkids once in awhile. And it's a great self-confidence booster for the little ones when Grandpa catches them doing something right! We have found this works well when kids are little.

Start Early. We know a lot of

you will have a problem with the, "you need to start when they are really young" strategy. Honestly, no new mother with a 3-month-old breast feeding infant is thinking ahead to "when this baby hits three, she's going to take over toilet scrubbing duty."

The reality is more like one mom who said to her 14-year-old daughter, "Get in there and clean up that pigsty, and don't come out until it's done—or until you turn 18—whichever comes first!" But if kids are not suitably trained at some point at least, it may be the illogical equivalent of saying, "Go drive a car" or "Go make a pie"— neither of which can be successfully done without a fair amount of guidance. Kids' rooms are actually a pretty complex task. Bed making, vacuuming and dusting require large motor skills, while folding clothes, straightening the desk and folding or hanging clothes on a hanger require some pretty refined small motor muscle dexterity.

So we need to spend some time with our kids to teach these proficiencies, and do it over and over. But most of us get so tangled up in our daily living—expediting everything, and coping with the frenetic pace—that

we largely ignore the importance of consistency in teaching household and life skills at very early ages. Yet, only those competencies that we or somebody else teaches and follows through on will work! Don't give up— and don't do it for them!

Teaching children self-gratification delay through the medium of household upkeep actually begins right about the time they can hold small objects in their hands. Even in small tasks like putting matching shoes together, returning building blocks to their containers, dropping their own dirty diapers in the trash and re-shelving books, you can begin to effect change and teach self-discipline in your child as early as age one. "If they can walk or chew gum,

they are ready to help!" said one dad.

Kids are practically born wanting to squirt, bat, swish, brush, rub, and play in water and suds. We need to let them experience all of these things, and match the action to cleaning in a positive way. For example, give them a small scrubber to wipe down suds following their bubble bath. Hand over an old toothbrush for scrubbing around the base of the bathroom faucet, following play with a little sink-sized tug boat. If the kids feel like everyone enjoys cleaning, and everybody is talking in kind, cooperative voices, they will follow suit.

Consistency Counts. In all fairness, there are some tasks kids just aren't going to like to do, and will never like to do. I have one who loves to mop and another who doesn't mind doing toilets a bit. Still another who would rather mow lawns and wash cars. Just like parents have their preferences (my sister Janet vacuums every spare moment she has), as much as we can organize it, let the kids do 90% of what they really like to do. As long as they are contributing to the greater good and putting in their hours, let's not absolutely demand that they do

things they mostly hate. (Why force-feed peas when they can only stomach

---

Basic principles for matching jobs to the age:

1. Don't expect kids to do all the work in the house. Aim to get *some* of the work done.
2. How many jobs? One idea is the child's age divided by two: age 12 does 6 jobs. Round up if needed.
3. Don't assign chores beyond the child's capability, or excessive numbers, or assign them as punishments, or give them in demeaning ways
4. Consider, evaluate, and balance all the other activities that kids are involved in: their music lessons, sports practices, homework, church, etc., so you don't overload chores.

---

carrots? Feed the peas to somebody else! All the vegetables will eventually get eaten.) This is a "do what you 'love' all the time, but do what you 'hate' only occasionally" mindset.

The more consistent parents are in ensuring this continuity of whatever tasks the children are practicing, the greater the increase of self-control skills emerging in the child will be. Parents, don't fail here. Kids are expecting we'll give in and give up.

Activate the senses. This one bit of personal counsel is worth this whole book. It's free, easy, and it works! Remember when you were a kid on cooking, baking or canning day at your home? The pleasant smells permeated the whole house. They almost pulled you in from outdoor play. Equally pleasant for me was the smell of Saturday morning housecleaning. I recall my mother waxing the kitchen floor with the fruity smell of Johnson's paste wax. Although it was quite the physical ritual, she hummed and smiled as she did it, so I never assumed it was any kind of drudgery at all. In fact, I was delighted on those work days, because I knew what was to follow. All of us kids got to put on thick wooly socks—mated or not—and skate back and forth across the linoleum until it glistened. Mom praised all of our good efforts as we polished.

Then there was the acrid smell of Clorox that whiffed up from the laundry basement; but it meant clean, white clothes were coming so I associated it as a positive. And I

certainly never minded filling my arms with the rows of towels and sheets dried outside on our clothes line. (Most kids don't even know what a clothes line is anymore.) That sun-soaked aroma filled my nostrils then, and added to my pleasant housekeeping memories now.

Don has been questioned, if not criticized, for his overboard passion for work and disinterest in play and partying. He attributed two possible elements to this "warped" view—first, As a youth,"I never, ever remember going to bed without knowing what we were going to be doing the next day— brand cattle, weed, bean, overhaul the combine, pick spuds, paint the barn, go fishing—no surprises." Second, "As we hooked up the teams, gassed the tractor, sharpened tools, and headed for the field, my father would break into song and joyfully talk to the cows as we passed them. He'd stop and sniff the air—he never did that when going to a movie or hunting, but always when he began any chore. Yes, we sang to cows while milking and talked to the horses while they pulled the raker and wagon. Work was never work. It was a delightful adventure." Don still hums when headed to clean toilets, strip floors, or climb a ladder. He actually sings out loud as he vacuums.

What's happened to all these rich household experiences that kids used to learn from? For starters, American kids' housework time has dropped 30% since the early 1980's. The new century finds most things done for us. We have automatic sprinklers, Roto-tillers, leaf blowers, snow blowers, pitching machines, dishwashers, dryers, power saws, power screwdrivers, and remote controls to tune the TV. One man quipped that before TV remotes were invented, people had more children so they could use them to change the stations! Automation has eliminated hundreds of duties we once could share with our children. Consequently, we must tax our most creative brain center to think of work experiences, routines, traditions, smells, and tastes that will create feelings that make pleasant housekeeping memories for our children.

For example, a few years ago my 11-year-old son entered his produce in the local community harvest show, and won some ribbons. He was delighted. Gardening means a good time for kids because it is 1) out of doors, 2) they get to use a few adult-style tools, 3) play in the dirt, and 4) do something magic. Things seem to appear out of nowhere, especially weeds! Look at garden catalogues or go to the local nursery and together decide and choose those plants that will work in your climate. Big seeds are generally easiest for kids to handle. You can also toss in a few "magic" vegetables like blue potatoes, yellow watermelons (they exist!), and white cucumbers that don't require any peeling.

Cooking, gardening, and cleaning activities need to be happening in our homes on a much more regular basis. These experiences will stimulate the senses in positive, familiar ways. Even if it's just one morning or one evening a week—do whatever you can to create those pleasant memories kids will associate with work and good family times. If you can't cook from scratch, at least let your child make Pillsbury cut and bake cookies with you. Or spray the kitchen floor with some of the wonderful cherry or almond-scented neutral cleaners, and Swiffer away—each with your own mop! Small investments like these will build mountains of confidence and positive sensory associations with housework now and later on. Plus it gives us opportunities to teach the right way of doing things, versus any way to cook, garden, and clean, etc.

Most common kid clutter

Simplify the Surroundings of the child. Work with them to declutter

Categories:

- Sentimental – stuffed animals, blankets
- School work
- Books
- Clothes (they've grown out of, or that they don't like)
- Socks (stretched out and mismatched)
- Games and puzzles
- Duplicates and extras (toys, linens, pillows, bedding)

Declutter and assign addresses. In our thrust to get everything up to a household standard, we need to be sure we don't make our children feel incapable of making their rooms look great, when their nemesis might just be too much stuff to wade through and organize. When television invaded our lives about 60 years ago, clutter moved in with it. The advertisers told us we needed more, so we bought it. Our multiple cars got squeezed out of standard garages fast-food diets our bodies, and malls took our money. Our lives became cluttered, complex and complicated.

Even when my kids were young, my standard gift request for birthdays, Mother's Day or Christmas was always, "I don't need anything; I'd be happy if everybody just got along." In spite of my resistance, with their father's support they usually came up with a few little gift items that were needed and appreciated. Now that my children are grown and have children of their own, they truthfully complain, "There really isn't anything Mom needs anymore!" Their father ran out of back-up gift ideas about the same time VCR tapes went out of vogue. After nearly six decades, I have accumulated all that I need.

Conversely, it's a phenomenon of our affluent society that adults nowadays hardly know what to buy for their own young kids for the same reason—they have it all. One grandmother complained that she didn't know what to get or do for a pre-teen granddaughter's birthday, because her parents had already provided it all—the entertainment, clothes, activities, technologies and trips. "What do I have left to give or do for my grandchild that can bond us, or that's unique or special?" Most of our children prosper and are privileged—even those who live in families of lesser means. Kids don't just get nutritious food at each meal; we back-up it with vitamins—then make sure they have their immunizations! They are cultured with dance and voice lessons. They have athletic training in little league, gymnastics and community sports. We provide computers and cars for high school and tutors and study-abroad experiences in college. Immediacy has become the standard and there is little delay or discipline in purchases or activities, no matter the age of the child.

This affluence and drive toward accumulation creates a household disease we call "stuffocation" in every room.

Take the bedroom for example. Most of them are <u>not</u> set up to function well for optimum daily living to begin with. They are crowded with excess belongings, furniture, and decorative memorabilia. What shelves and drawers they do have, are not conducive to being used for needed items. This is problematic. 1) Children have too many toys and clothes (Don says 75% more than they use) and 2) They need user-friendly storage places that are more easily accessible and designed for easier pick up at the end of the day.

Kids only use about 20% of their toys 80% of the time. Talk with your child about his favorites and move all else out of his active storage and shelving space into a Toy Library. Some call this a toy rotation or alternation approach, but it simply means moving less used or extra toys into less accessible areas. This way, remaining toys don't have to be sorted through each time they are looking for their favorite. Kids will also stay more in command of their room if they have an address (physical place) for each remaining item. Picking up and cleaning up will be infinitely easier forever after. Every month or so, rotate some of the stored toys back into active use.

There should be an actual "address" for our clothes, dishes, books, and every other household item that we have multiples of—as well as the toys. Just as every family member knows that the fridge is the "home" for cold things, and the medicine cabinet is where all aspirin and cold medicines "live," so should they also know exactly where every article of clothing and each book and game resides. Typically childrens' belongings should live in drawers, on shelves and hang from rods. Think

---

Why is clutter bad:

1. Stuff takes space and insulates us from each other
2. Makes us late, lose things, frustrated (lost shoes; favorite animal)
3. Complicates our cleaning (moving and re-arranging)
4. Disorder invites more disorder— mess perpetuates itself

---

about it—order is simply necessity in place!

It's just easier to do it myself. Mothers don't do their children or their husbands any favors if they constantly clean up after them. There is no teaching of being responsible for one's own actions if we are omnipresent to clean up and fix up everything that is out of line. We have a great training ground for life right under our noses if we'll use it. Anyone old enough to mess up is old enough to clean up. Our children and our spouses, and all of us are responsible for our own mess, whether it's financial, health related, moral, emotional, legal, or having to do

> Clutter is one of the chief causes of family fights.
> *—Better Homes and Gardens*

with a relationship. We all need to be responsible to fix up what we mess up.

Without taking over your child's responsibilities, change roles once in awhile. Don't let some routine home tasks get stuck in concrete unless kids like it that way. Dads can bake and make beds, the middle-aged child can do laundry and arrange flowers, Mom can wash the car, and sister can trim the bushes. Let the kids feel like they are in charge, by letting them divvy up family tasks occasionally.

Again, the main thing is to involve the kids in the cleaning process. If they make mess, they need to know they must also clean it up. If we always clean off our kids' dinner plates, make their beds, wash their clothes, scrub their toilets, section their grapefruits, and trim their nails, they aren't likely to become domestically, personally, OR socially responsible. There's simply no teaching of being responsible for one's own actions if we are always present to fix everything that is out of line.

> "The motivation to redecorate my room was a great tool for making me want to clean. It gave me a sense of ownership and that was probably when I wanted to clean my room the most."
>
> –Natalee P.

Just like you can't exercise and eat broccoli for other people to make their bodies healthy, or attend church and say their prayers for them to instill spiritual sensitivity, and you can't keep an open door policy on your wallet if you hope to make children financially savvy. Likewise, most kids can give more than what their parents expect out of them around home. We need to remember that we're raising more than a family pet that is enjoyed but not expected to work — we are raising a child who is part of a family home improvement team.

When kids build, overhaul, sew, paint, invent, or whittle, they are going to create some mess. Yes, cooking, bathing, having pets, and pursuing crafts and projects all mean messes. It's part of life and often the bigger the mess, the bigger the blessing. The problem is not in making a mess, but in leaving it behind for someone else to fix.

Cleaning up after another person reinforces bad behavior. It's really more of an effective way to inflict long-term punishment on a person you don't like—but it's not something you want to do to your child!

Do it for them too many times, and they will let you forever...

When Boy Scouts go camping, they had better be prepared for some cold weather. Don told his scouts to bring with a coat no matter what the weather forecast. Knowing that kids seldom listen, he threw in a couple of extra coats, just in case. The coats were both needed that night. Next scout camp, five scouts needed coats. Because they thought Don would have whatever they needed, they made less effort to take care of themselves and bring the coats along. Suddenly, the extra coats stopped! One half dozen frozen boys learned a lesson. After two more hikes (and hopefully forever after), they brought with their own outer wear!

A respected octogenarian named Thomas Monson cautioned parents to "...share household duties. It is often easier to do everything yourself than to persuade your children to help, but it is so essential for them to learn the importance of doing their share.... Don't indulge them to excess for they must learn to make their own way in the world."

The mechanics of clean rooms. Jobs will vary depending on how big your home is, how many kids you have, how much stuff you have, and how clean you like your home to be.

How to divvy up the jobs. Decide in a family meeting what jobs need doing by whom. Parents should first list out everything to be done, so there is no guesswork or mental telepathy as to what needs fixing or maintaining. And remember, it's not Mom's house or Dad's house, it's *our* house that we are working on.

A comprehensive list of chores allows the kids to see the enormity of the job, and thus feel more responsibility. Include all things age appropriate, and even such incidentals as putting newspapers in the recycle bin, clipping coupons, freshening the dog's water, delivering mail to household members, changing toilet paper, straightening the silverware drawer and so on. Next comes the delegating of assignments—which will help them feel responsibility and ownership. Be firm, fair, and flexible. Just like the parent's paycheck is budgeted to meet family temporal needs, divide up the chores. Put a star by any non-negotiable or transferable jobs like—

- Make bed (all)
- Baking in oven, microwave or stovetop (mom and dad must supervise)
- Drive car on errands (parents and teens with driver licenses only)
- Pick up toys (child)

There's no need to specify boy and girl jobs. Each child should learn how to do everything he is capable of doing.

Beware of giving jobs to just the oldest or best workers; otherwise, distribute household jobs according to age, availability and ability.

Write up the schedule for one week, then one month. Modify as needed and repeat. I used this method for including my eight children in daily household tasks over the 22-year period we raised them. Today each of them can do most things with some degree of confidence. They are masters at organizing and I think their favorite job still is to dejunk our attic (especially my stuff!). For sure they have positive attitudes, and feel a responsibility to equally help their mates in homes of there own. That being said, don't assume that every day or even every hour will go perfectly.

For example, I pulled out a family schedule from years ago when my children were ages 1, 3, 5, 7, 9, 11, 13, and 15-years-old. On that week's assignment sheet I put a little indicator number from "1" to "10" by each day, marking it as a bad or good day. Tuesday started out with a great score of "10"; then the week slipped incrementally downward: Wednesday, "8"; Thursday, "7"; Friday, "6"; and

Saturday, "5." Sunday inched up to a "7" again. I'm not sure if any objective criteria were used in assigning these numbers, but we obviously weren't a perfect, all-together family all the time! Still, the system worked for us most of the time. We were a team and I guided and praised their effort and success as we improved together. Shadow parenting eventually paid off with a cleaner home, and kids that possibly developed greater mastery of self. Most importantly, the children learned that when they made a mess they had to clean it up. That same principle has carried over into their adult lives. When they mess up with grades, money, food, or choices, they are the ones responsible to fix it.

Tummies need filling. It's best to feed the body before you feed the soul. When you get ready to organize your family's master schedule, to include calendaring and household work assignments, kids will always be more calm and apt to listen if planning sessions come after a fun meal.

Each September, about two weeks after school started, we bought a bunch of canned root beers and ordered several large pizzas. My family then gathered at my husband's office and eat our picnic feast around his big conference table. Afterward, we were ready to discuss the upcoming school-year schedule. (Family meetings can be held at beaches, parks, or even in your back yard. But pick some place that's different than usual, so that the experience is unique.) After we devoured the pizza, we calendared.

Child after child gave their best shot at what looked to be upcoming months' activities now that they were back in classes. We then factored in sports practices, music lessons and church obligations. Next we matched household tasks to kids' abilities and available schedules. We proceeded

> According to a University of Toronto Study, chores encourage compassion and sensitivity. Kids who have routine chores are more likely to be considerate of others than those who don't. They express thoughtfulness in spontaneous acts, like comforting someone who's sad, or lending a hand without being asked.

around the table (there were 10 of us), and let each child, along with the parents, take their pick of favorite jobs within their age group category. I usually made sure one of the boys had toilet cleaning duty, as it always helped him refine his aim (which often took up to 8 years to perfect). Eventually, just like at an estate auction, all the jobs were assigned and the kids were content.

> "Chores build self-reliance and self-esteem by showing kids their work has value," (Positive Discipline by Jane Nelsen, Ed.D.) Chores boost a child's sense of "social significance" and family contribution, promoting cooperation, teamwork and empathy.

Children feel more secure and gain comfort from predictability such as a family schedule. Sure adjustments had to be made down the road, but it was a beginning. It gave us a sense of order, and a level of serenity for each child to know what was expected. They would be accountable for certain things which in turn, obligated them to be more self-disciplined. There was little time left for television, though we always made sure they had time for free play.

Kid's cleaning tools and techniques. Cleaning can actually be therapeutic. When we see a room that's organized, a counter that shines, a bathroom that smells good, and a closet that's neat, we smile. Happy people are more healthy than people who are not. And to get our rooms in a gleaming state, we need some good tools to start with.

- Kids should have their own little cleaning caddy.
- Make sure they have <u>clean cloths</u>—not those hardened rags left over from washing the car; and they should be sized to easily wring out with small hands.
- Many of the new disposable, <u>cleaning wipes</u> can be effective and appropriate for older children to use. Be alert to cautions on product packaging.
- A <u>firm toothbrush</u> or denture brush will be just right for their smaller hands to use on intricate cleaning jobs such as ornate handles and bases of faucets.

- Telescoping dusters can help shorter kids reach higher places.

One lady we heard of told her husband and son that vacuuming is indoor mowing. Since men like things with motors and wheels, perhaps that tactic will work at least a time or two!

Scale equipment to size of child. A while ago, Home and Garden Channel's "Smart Solutions" program asked me to do a segment on inspiring kids to clean. I interviewed my own children as well as some neighborhood friends and tasked them to come up with their top ways to get children "just begging" to clean. Actually, no approach will motivate any child to beg to clean—save those under age 4 perhaps—but I did get some good ideas. At the top of the list was to scale cleaning equipment down to kid-size. For example, use a sand bucket or ice-cream pail for mopping chores, and cut about a foot off the top of an old mop handle to make it more manageable. Another good idea was to put window cleaner in a squirt gun, equip the child with some paper towel and let him have a show down with a sibling on the opposite side of the window. The challenge?

They've got to finish all the windows before their squirt gun empties.

Some companies have kid-sized cleaning sets with small ironing boards, actual irons that spray water (but no heat), brooms, mops, scrub brushes and realistic vacuums that make sounds. All of these items are healthy and fun for little hands that are learning to mimic what they see their parents do. Dr. Stevanne Auerback of www.drtoy.com says that kids spend time playing with toys because "It's a way to explore and practice budding, yet still undeveloped roles and interests." How better than to offer scaled-down cleaning toys that help them imitate what their parents do. Don suggests using adult-size real tools as soon as they are able.

After waiting for more than a year to visit grandma, young J, Sam, and Knox had barely gotten through the door of my house when they headed straight for the small-sized cleaning brooms, mop, dustpan, vacuum and duster in my pantry area. Their mother says they love to clean because, "we always do it together and they love mimicking their mom!"

Color Code your kids. Well, not actually the kid, but everything they use that's washable. Particularly if you have more than one child, assign a set color and use it several ways. When bath, hand and wash cloths land on the floor, it's easy to figure out who let it drop. I assigned towel colors to my kids for years, and it really fetters out the guilty parties in a hurry. You may also want bed sheets to be in the same color family for each person, or for each size/type of bed. It just makes sorting things out after the laundry a whole lot easier.

For Christmas last year, I gave all eight of my grandchildren their own fluffy, thirsty, color-coded bath towel with their name monogrammed right on the bottom of it. I also gave the children a sleepover slumber bag with their name embroidered along the edge. As children learn to recognize their names on personal items, they also tend to assume a little more stewardship.

When my family of ten was all living at home, we went through about 70 pairs of socks each week. There were plain just not enough different kinds of socks being sold at the department store to buy something different for each of the six boys—so I tacked on short pieces of yarn to the toes in identifying colors that aided in mating and distributing.

My family likes the color-code idea even today, with paper-cup holders matched to the last four people at home. They are assigned as follows: Sandi, red; Reed, green; Eden, pink and Ricky, blue. Each person sticks to his or her assigned color all day so there's less dishwashing.

Make the bed easier. Take off the casters so the bed is low. Teach the child, before he or she gets out of bed in the morning, to pull the covers up to their chin, then slip out of the side without disturbing the covers too much. That way the bed is almost made, because they just need to tuck the spread over the pillow! If the bed must be up against a wall, pin the bedding to the mattress on the wall side with several large-sized diaper pins. This way, even young children can pull the covers over sideways for an easy, smooth fit. Lastly, consider having just a fitted sheet on the bottom, and a fluffy, washable comforter on the top. That's it! No extra sheets or blankets in between to struggle with. With just one cover to pull into place, you might actually start seeing something besides a huge pile of covers with a mattress somewhere under it.

Make small things easier to clean. If your kids have a collection of small objects, like spoons, thimbles, ceramic animals, dolls, trophies, whistles or a hundred other things, display them on a simple tray so the items can easily be moved all together for dusting, or to alternate locations.

Use wall space for storage as much as possible. Any time you can suspend an item, do it! It's one less thing to have to knock over, move around or vacuum under. Shelving can hold a multitude of items that might otherwise end up on the floor.

My mother-in-law, for example, built a high, shallow shelf around the entire parameter of her family room. Along it she displayed several hundred unique salt and pepper shakers she had collected over the years from different people and locations around the world. The collection was low enough to be seen and enjoyed (certainly a great conversation piece), but high enough that they didn't need to be dusted more than once a year—because you simply couldn't see the actual display shelf itself.

If you have a collection that is in the dozens or hundreds, and each item is small in size, you might want to consider such a wall application.

When you choose open shelving units to hold your child's books or toy tubs or containers, think about bringing additional units to extend along an entire wall. I did this for one of our daughters who was especially prone to stacking (dropping) her clean laundry

> "...kids raised in clean homes—regardless of their intellectual ability or parents' household income—stick with school longer and earn more money as adults than those raised with dust bunnies."
> —University of Michigan School of Social Work

on her bedroom carpet. Seems it was just too much extra effort to open each drawer, put the correct article in; or hang item by item in the closet. In short order the piles of clean clothes got mixed in with the dirty. Because kids hate any extra effort or movement to put their things away, allow them to place clean clothes on open shelves! My daughter had one 4-shelf unit devoted to swim suits, cover-ups, pants, shorts and underclothes; another unit held all her blouses, sweaters, socks and pj's. Two others stocked books, stationery, pictures and what-knots. It was really quite an attractive arrangement that didn't detract from the room at all—and it was a much greater incentive to put clothing away right after things were cleaned and folded. The floor could be vacuumed much faster, too!

Build in as much as possible in childrens' rooms. When Don's children were young he built a miniature stagecoach in their room. It was inexpensive and cut cleaning way down. Besides being a great place to play, it had a built-in clothes closet, toy box and hamper, and two nearby built-in beds with storage drawers underneath. This really reduced the places to litter or leave anything.

When furnishings are built in they can't be disarranged or tipped over, and there are far fewer exposed edges and corners for kids to get hurt on. Audio and video equipment and computer workstations are excellent things to build in, too.

In my home, I created a "magic door way" in the back part of one of the bedroom closets. This secret access was super easy to build and cost almost nothing. It connected two rooms, and gave the kids hours of hide-and-seek, cops and robbers, and catch-me-if-you-can play options.

Wall hang or suspend all that you can. Anything you can get up

> "Educational experts have found through the years that organizing toys and props make a child's environment more conducive to learning, creativity and free play,"
> —Home Management 101 by Debbie Williams

W.O.R.K. (Wonderful Opportunities for Responsible Kids)

To make kids happy helpers we must establish a work ethic. How?
- Write out tasks, or show pictures rather than issue verbal assignments
- Label, label, label. This reminds kids where everything goes
- Carpet kids' floors. It makes things quieter. Vacuuming is easier for kids than using a broom and mop.
- The floor can be patterned to hide spills and stains, and it's slip proof so it's more safe.
- Think outside the toy box… Put their play things in individual containers
- Keep lids off trash and laundry baskets
- Provide washable furniture
- Finish walls in scrubbable wallpaper or washable satin finish paint
- Place a bulletin board (chalk, dry erase, cork) on one wall
- Make it easier – like less covers on the bed, fewer belongings to straighten and sort through
- Make or buy cleaning tools kid-sized
- Box up or suspend or get rid of extra stuffed animals, unused and extra toys
- Remove all clothing that is not currently being worn
- Discard all broken toys, games and puzzles with missing parts or duplicates
- Provide plenty of shelving and lowered rod space
- Attach hooks to backs of doors
- Fix up all their things in the active space, so they are easily usable
- Put all belongings in logical places so that everything has its own home
- If kids have collections, keep them wall mounted or on rotating shoe shelves
- Adjust the vacuum to the "high" carpet setting making it easier to use

off the floor, do it! When the place where something belongs is clearly established, easy to reach and easy to use, it encourages things to be put back rather than strewn around. Even hang the trash can on a wall bracket. It's easy to sweep or vacuum under and it never gets tipped over. Install pegs to hang knapsacks purses, book bags, and duffel bags on. With just one effortless movement, an item can be stored off the floor.

Finally, don't be too impressed by what you see in kid bedroom sections of "Glitzy Homes and Gardens" or "Good House Copying" magazines. Most of the kids' rooms in these displays are for show, not for sharing and functioning in.

As children learn to organize their rooms, they will transfer these skills to other areas in the home. They will also have more skill and confidence in organizing and completing everything from schoolwork to music lessons and into college, the career world, and their own family life.

Conclusion. Once our children are trained in specifics, we need to be consistent in expecting the tasks be done before other activities. Next, they need to know that what they do is appreciated—that good behaviors

pay off. Our communication must be centered on praise, hope, expectation and approval. We must nurture their best natures and turn on the kid instead of the television. Soon they will see (and parents will see), that the more successful they are in controlling the surroundings over which they have stewardship, the more successful they will be in other areas of their lives.

As we are consistent in teaching and expecting that housekeeping duties be done— we will have a cleaner house for sure, but beyond that, our children will be on the road to adult responsibility. They will see the positive extensions of service, cleanliness and organization. They will be more inclined to delay gratification. Their airier, cleaner rooms and habitations will produce a calmer inner spirit as they work and live.

Don't do it for them—and don't give up.

> Children who live in clean homes tend to do better in school—and in their careers, as adults

Ways to teach cleaning to children:

- Have a positive attitude
- Although there are regularly assigned jobs, occasionally substitute a new job requiring a new skill
- Limit time to do chores
- Limit number of toys they play with at a time
- Don't make expectations so high kids get discouraged about pleasing
- Make it fun-turn on the music
- Have friends clean with them
- Work together as a team whenever you can, but especially on the harder jobs
- Don't make it a punishment

- Be firm, consistent; don't let them negotiate out of it
- Be fair – their personal room should not need to be cleaner than the rest of the house—nor should it be dirtier
- Be patient and tolerant. Jobs done by children will seldom be up to adult standards
- Be specific in job expectations
- Chores can be too simple or too few—stretch so they learn, but not overwhelm.
- Don't rush when you're working with children

Section 3: Teen Clean Machines

Parents may not dare vocalize it, but more than a few of us anxiously await that daunting time when our young adult children leave home to be on their own! "Maybe they'll finally learn what life is all about!" we silently say as we smirk. Will that first electric bill put them into shock, or will it be doing all their own laundry, filling their car with gas they bought, cleaning toilets they dirtied, buying their own clothes, preparing meals, or fixing the flat tire?

We know it's entirely appropriate that these life experiences be handed off to them—it's a *right of passage* routine—and it's just a smidgen delightsome. This moment in family history will also inaugurate parents' empty-nest life of more time, more money, and reclaimed storage space! (When did they get all those belongings that fill every extra shelf, closet and drawer in our homes?) Common storage spaces seemed to attract their clutter like lint in a dryer.

Right on the heels of this greatly anticipated blissful launch, an unexpected panic sets in!

While the prospect of their moving out will most certainly eliminate the perpetual disorder they have created in our own homes, will slovenliness transfer smack into their new apartments, quarters, dorms, and condos? Perish the thought!

Is there any time or intelligent ammo left for one last ditch, give-it-all-you-have, desperate, do-or-die effort to correct their weak spots in housekeeping responsibility?

A few parents pray that some unidentified *other person* out there will step up and fix their kid's mess problem (the same kid they have had little to no effect on for 18+ years). Perhaps the new roommate, employer, professor, staff sergeant, co-worker, missionary companion, friend, fiancé, spouse, or in-law—will have a more positive and productive effect on straightening out their personal habits than the parent ever had. And in some cases, this does happen—but reality says, "Good luck!"

When required or expected, only a fair percentage of our kids actually behave better and get neater once out on their own. Even so, during those last few years they are under our wings for their final chapter of nurturing—if we can have a good effect—we'll feel less guilty dumping them on some rescuer. Because once they leave, they are 95% out of our circle of influence—though never out of our circle of concern.

Is it possible to train and teach our OLDER ADOLESCENTS to do house-hold chores?

For as long as parents have been rearing teens, you'd think someone would have figured out just the right brilliant scientific strategy for how to eliminate the classic littered bedroom and dirty bathroom condition in our homes, especially with all the talk show behaviorist doctors chiming in. Why haven't we broken the messy cycle? If kids can put numbers in the right order for college calculus, why can't they put their rooms in order? One daughter's room got so messy, her mom told me she was never sure if she was in there or not! The mom's only consolation, "One day my daughter will have her own children just like her." Touché.

Humans and animals coddle and preserve their young to a fault, not wanting them to taste of grief or discomfort. Today's kids are more looked after (and for a longer time) than ever before. We give them everything they need and most things they want. Sometimes we even try to insulate them from real world earning opportunities, fearing it will hinder their social potential.

So kids grow up, expecting more and more—sometimes beyond the parent's ability to keep up. It's offspring entitlement epidemic. In spite of our parenting missteps, however, in many respects teens today are the absolute sharpest generation yet. They are intellectual, savvy and healthy. But do they reciprocate our nurturing protection and attention by happily doing household tasks to help maintain the family unit?

NOT IF THEY CAN HELP IT!

One woman who teaches freshman composition at a university assigned her students to write on the topic, "How Would I Raise My Children Differently from the Way My Parents Raised Me?" She expected them to complain about how much parents were on kids' backs about things; however, 97% of her students said they wished their parents had given them "more responsibility." Further, most of them believed they were now "slobs" because they were never taught how to do simple household tasks. Hmmm.

Apparently their sophisticated arsenal of convincing arguments to get out of every perceived morsel of work must be a smoke screen! They really want to help out—parents just haven't learned the right approach to get them to buy in.

SO...What are the excuses?

It's not cool. Why would any teen want to have a room that looks a lot different than any of his friends? They are all about sameness with each other, and differentiation from their immediate family. Since most friends have messy rooms and bathrooms, it stands to reason they want to fit that model. This same mindset is mirrored in their clothing. The style of their apparel mimics their rooms—messy, raggedy, faded, tattered, frayed, and holey. These are "in" items at school. Kids slouch around in thrift store discards because it's cool...as in the breeze blows through the holes in the legs, butt and thigh sections of whatever is hanging on their bodies. Shabby clothes, shabby rooms.

Low self-esteem. Psychologists tell us that some kids purposefully keep their room full of clutter and disarray because they want recognition. They feel crummy, disorganized and in great turmoil on the inside, and want to let the world know that they feel just like their room looks. They are calling out to everybody that life is not going well for them. Their self-esteem is as low as their pile of junk is high.

To express control. How many ways do teens interact with their parents? Not a lot these days. We seldom travel together as they grow older, because many kids get their own cars as soon as they get their driver licenses—or they drive with their friends who have licenses. Most teens cringe at thought of *family* trips—unless their friend tags along. At home, we eat very few meals together, and seldom do projects or clean together. So how do they get some interaction and attention? Some push parents' hot button by letting their rooms go to the

dogs. Dogs mark their territory just as kids mark their own small sanctuaries. The Bible tells us that man is a natural enemy to God; likewise kids may be a natural enemy to parental control—or at least to the perceived authority. Thus, the messy room.

We must also be reminded that teens have an instinctive drive to get their independence any way they can. Their private room, whether it's perfectly clean, or pitifully dirty, is a perfect venue to set them apart from the rest family—in positive or negative ways.

No productive energy left over. Yep, some kids seem born lazy—but nearly every teen we know just plain likes or needs to sleep a lot. A few are

still growing, and most all of them like to stay out late and run hard. It's interesting how we tell nighttime stories to our toddlers to get them to go to sleep; then when kids hit puberty and go on dates, they begin telling us stories that keep us awake all night!

Besides the organized sports, music and required studies, teens like to do a thousand optional things—room cleaning not usually being one of them. They watch television, surf the Internet, instant message, play video games, talk on cell phones and hang with friends. They make themselves exhausted. When you combine a tired teen with a species that is extraordinarily skilled at procrastination—well, you have major room Cleaning Avoidance Disorder, or CAD (and if we make it a disease, it isn't their fault because you <u>catch</u> a disease!)

It takes too much valuable time. Even if teens did not have schedules that were completely filled, they would certainly not want to waste a minute straightening or cleaning their surroundings. Cleaning is, well, a hard sell. It seems so repetitive, and there's so little return—definitely not the best way to spend a Saturday morning. And what's the point or advantage of all that effort expended cleaning, when it only stays looking good for hours—maybe even minutes—and the mess is smack back in your face. "Smart kids" reason that there's certainly lots better things to do.

Fear. What will they uncover or dislodge if they take the leap, and do that really deep cleaning one day? The thought of discovery may be a genuine deterrent for some of our faint-hearted adolescents. For example, I grew up in a musty basement bedroom. I lived in perpetual fear of finding the big tiger spider, or even a baby frog, that somehow worked its way in through the window well and took refuge in my clothes. Once my things hit the floor, I was afraid to pick them up—either to

> Mind-set matters: Be careful what you call cleaning, dejunking and organizing. Is it always housework or can we occasionally refer to it as home improvement? If it's always the miserable, ultimate punishment, it will be an eternal negative to the family.

re-hang or to wash.

Later on, my family had a medium-sized pet corn snake that slithered out of its cage one day. We were all on high alert, fearful that we would find him taking refuge in our shoes or between our bed sheets. It was certainly not an incentive for doing deep cleaning any time soon. Weeks later we found him plenty alive, snuggled down in a silky swimsuit in the summer storage closet.

Other room-cleaning-avoidance categories might be insects, field rodents or their tracks, spider webs, nests and roaches. All of these critters and their fallout discourage kids from cleaning. Are there *fear creatures* in your kids' rooms? And what about the "fear" of breaking a fingernail? Only in recent years have our teenage girls started getting expensive manicures and false nails that need to be protected!

Just too overwhelming. At some point there can plainly be too much of a landfill mess to even know where to start. When closets are bulging and drawers are unable to close—and outfits from several seasons and sizes ago lay 30" deep on the floor, it's just beyond teen mentality and ability to tackle. Their clean clothes have long

since mixed in with dirty clothes and have become "dirty by association." Kids need to see clean room results as quickly as they won their last computer game—with about the same amount of effort expended.

We all can understand their frustration. When I return from a 10-day business trip, and confront my own desk full of 3rd Class mail and unopened letters, notes, phone call messages and magazines, I don't hardly know where to start—except that I avoid facing up to it for at least a day or two. Or when my sink and counters overflow with dishes, pans and serving pieces following a big evening of entertainment, I'm not exactly inspired to jump in and put the mess in order. Adults have their own places and times of overload and so do our kids.

Cleaning tools and supply shortage. Under an inconvenient counter or in a dark cupboard or corner, a household maid caddy can sometimes be found. If not a caddy, perhaps a box, basket or bucket stuffed with some chemicals, tools and crunchy wrung out dried rags designated for family "cleaning" use. The whole arsenal of things usually stinks, and is a real turn-off for kids to touch or use. They figure it's plain safer and less disgusting not to get involved.

No cleaning skills. For households who do stock all the right cleaning stash, in the perfect caddy or cart, even 18 to 22-year olds don't know which product is for which cleaning job. No kid is going to spend time reading the directions on the back of each cleaner. It's pretty common knowledge that the blue cleaner is for glass and windows, but how do you apply it--with newspapers, paper towel, or terry hand towels? The other colored chemicals are anybody's guess. What to do for the toilet is the biggest turn-off, and therefore it's least likely to ever, ever get cleaned. Even if they did decide to clean it, they seldom know the best method.

No improvement in sight. Sometimes, even after serious picking up and cleaning up, our kids' rooms look about the same. They put out mega effort for minuscule return. The real problem here: we haven't provided enough shelving to hold all the folded clothes. Desk and drawer space is inadequate to store books, papers and mail; and there's inadequate closet rod

hanging space. It's not that our teen's effort is half-hearted, it's just that there's no feasible way to organize all they own in the physical structure of the room they live in.

Too Much Stuff "TMS." No argument here; most of our children have over-accumulation virus which might be the No. 1 social disease of the 21st Century. It creates more turmoil and tension between family members

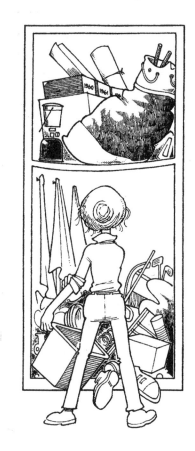

than just about any other malady. When family members can't find what they want to read, watch, wear, or listen to, we get nasty with each other. Sports things, clothes, CDs and DVDs get traded around until nobody is sure what belongs to anybody. Possessions get buried, broken, lost, needlessly replaced, and improperly cared for. Any available horizontal surface is the first target for these extra accumulations. Next, closets become bloated. In the final stages, stuffocation of the entire open breathing space sets in.

Not my problem. I was frustrated that none of my children seemed to be taking responsibility for cleaning up community mess areas of our home. If it wasn't in their bedroom, it wasn't their problem. Thus the commonly shared family newspaper, magazines, snack dishes, towels, umbrellas, lap blankets and so on, seldom got put away or straightened up. One day, my husband and I decided to try an experiment. We took a generic pillow from the linen closet and placed it in a busy doorway, right on the floor, smack between the family room and kitchen. There was no way any of the kids could walk around it. Their choices were either pick it up, or step over the pillow dozens of times each day as they came to meals, watched television or answered the front door. Well, they didn't just step over it, they broad jumped over it, time and again! It became a new family sport. I predicted that the pillow would "lie in state" for several days. **Wrong.** It was there for two weeks—which proves my theory that most kids take even less ownership and responsibility for things out of place in the general use areas of the house than they do with their personal things.

So…how do parents respond to all of these common excuses? First, we often complicate the whole matter by **over** or **under** reacting, and our tactics don't always inspire action for the right reasons. Let us share some examples.

How do we get kids to work?

First, the old familiar standbys:
1. **Malicious Obedience.** If they don't clean when, where or to what level we say, we give ultimatums or punishments. We know they have the ability to clean their rooms and

change their sheets, so when they don't respond to repeated threats, they get spanked (or given time outs) when they are young and *grounded* when they are older. They lose driving, phone and friend privileges. Their allowance gets docked. We yell, we demand, or we swear—and we seem to get results. This method is similar to that practiced in the military where a typical young man is inducted and immediately reports to boot camp for training. More than likely, his laundry, ironing, picking up, bed making and cooking have been done for him since childhood.

It's no surprise that right away his bunk and barracks look like a grenade detonated in his locker. The sergeant doesn't like what he sees so he takes action. Then, overnight and forever after, the private's personal space is pristine! What happened? It was the immediate punishment of a nine-mile run with rifle held in two hands, raised above his head! The young man was warned that from now on, every minute of every day, unless he is sleeping in it, his bed will be made with sheets tucked so tight that a dropped quarter

would bounce on it. His locker will be perfectly arranged—or else— another 9-miler. The discipline was decisive, complete and successful. A lifetime of sloppiness was corrected overnight, and practiced long enough to have a positive carryover, ideally for the rest of his life.

2. Bribery and leverages. At what point does an incentive to work become a bribe instead of a reward? True, it is a fine line, but generally bribes manipulate. Rewards encourage and guide. A bribe is still a gift, but it is extorted as an inducement to do what should already be done. Kids start to get the "what's in it for me" attitude if the incentive is too much, comes too frequently, or has no value to them. It then shifts over into the bribe category. When the focus is on the reward, the helpfulness is a means to an end. If a reward is the sole reason for behavior, it will need to become bigger and bigger to get the same kind of behavior. As this happens, it shifts over into bribe category and it is no longer a good incentive. For example, if my son takes me to the airport, and I pay him

$10 for taking two hours of his time to do it, it is a reward for his time. The next time he's needed to drop me off, if he says, "I don't want to unless I get $10," then the money is a manipulator and becomes a bribe. Those who don't have the militaristic inclination to force their children into obedience may resort to quid pro quo tactics. "If you clean up your room, I'll take you to the mall and buy you a dress," or "If you'll clean that dirty toilet I'll play basketball with you for 20 minutes."

It's an "if you do this…then I'll give you that," psychology. For some parents, the method works quite effectively, as children always

I cleaned up!

need or want something, and most parents have the resources to bargain for it. It is a drastic home maintenance plan that has muscle, but it builds bribery expectation. We have control over a plethora of things kids need: money, car, space, a signature, machines, passes, memberships, clothes, credit card, etc. If we use these to remind kids of the behavior we want, we may get some response. Many parents feel that prodding with bait is still better than letting them procrastinate to the bitter end. Remember, incentive generally runs out when money and bribes do. *When you have to coax kids with money or other "genuine" incentives to do something they are otherwise unwilling to do, it's a bribe.*

3. **Gracious groveling.** If we are especially desperate—like when unexpected company is due to show up, or we're stranded in a broken down car, or need to run to the emergency room with a sick younger child—we'll say and do almost anything to extract a promise of help.

We don't want to create a public scene or ignite a confrontation, but we don't want to let our kids off the hook if we are desperate for their help. When threats, bribes, incentives and other tactics don't work, some of us beg. Our youth have some sensitivity hidden behind their hurry, so at times they are reachable if we plead. We can put them on a powerful guilt trip when we need their help big time. A few will respond very agreeably to this method—if our crises have not been habitual. But do we really want this to happen?

How about a Clean Break from these three kinds of angles used to extract help!

We see some *fresh* ideas for our teen generation, with results that are much more positive and predictable.

Pass along the praise. Yes, even nearly grown kids will clean for admiration. Since most kids want to be well thought of by their extended family relatives and neighbors more than immediate family, encourage visits outside the home, often! When they return, you'll hear the parental report, "Your Nancee is the neatest girl I've

ever seen. Not a stitch of mess left behind anywhere, and she constantly asked me what she could do to help out. Boy, have you ever raised her right!" We look sideways at our Nancee to see if she has recently transformed into another child. Surely they aren't talking about our daughter—the one who keeps her own bedroom carpet perpetually clean by keeping it perpetually covered. Did the angel "More-organize" visit her en route to the friend's house? Nope. It's a phenomenon that when our kids see us clean, they learn the routine—just resist practicing it. But when they recognize a chance to help at somebody else's home, or at camp, or on a trip, they go gangbusters to please.

No one outgrows the need for praise. If we praise their cooking, they will cook more often and better. When we praise their practicing, they play more. We are quick to gawk at their hand-drawn Johnny Van Gogh pictures, we applaud our kids at musical performances and we leap to our feet when they score an athletic point. Let's show our elation when we find something clean, replaced, matched, folded, or organized. It also works wonders when they hear us brag to strangers, relatives, or friends about how well they do something.

Worthy rewards. Rewards encourage. When kids do something that is helpful such as service, or even achievement, we may reward them with time, money or an activity. A reward is something given as an acknowledgment of what they have done that is good. Parents give rewards for grades, work or other worthy goals that are reached. Rewards (or incentives) may need to change frequently so they don't slip over into becoming a bribe—and the sole reason for doing something. The focus is on the helpfulness, and the reward is a gift. These are offerings of material goods, allowance or privileges from parents to their kids. They can watch television, use the car or have friends over when assigned task(s) are done. There's no bribing, pleading or threats. They get a reward for a service, or they don't. We aren't playing desperate supervisor here, we're just giving them a chance to earn some needed money, time or a benefit. It is a boss-employee structured relationship. When you use money or other "genuine" incentives for chores, kids are willing to do it for a reward.

Assignment and expectation.

There are a few families whose kids do household chores without any reward or expectation in return. It's just what everybody in the family does, and what they've been doing since the family started. There are always the regular assignments like making the bed and picking up toys at night, but there's also a lot of extra things that come along which might be different every day. They do them all! Each person is simply trained to do what is needed, whether it's dishes on Friday, trash on Wednesday and/or laundry on Saturday. *Expectation* is an amazing motivator. These parents have learned to "relate" to their teens, not "control" them. If you started kids out

> Attitude rules: Moms continue to rule in most homes, even though dads carry much of the cooking and cleaning responsibility. She is the leader and sets the emotional and energy standard for the organization and work in most homes

young with this approach, it will likely continue to work without too much flak during the teen era. If not (which is the case with most of us probably), read on…

Set standards not schedules.
Some years ago, Don consulted with the Bell Telephone Company. Workers were to clean around 30,000 buildings. Originally managers presented him with a big, thickly bound book of directions called "specs" which not only specified *what* was to be cleaned, but *when*, and *how* (skills necessary). The specs spelled out every procedure — mopping, dusting, trash removal, and so on. The dilemma was the *frequency* requirement. Frequency says "clean the corner every Tuesday night." But what happens if a cockroach wanders in and dies in the corner on Wednesday morning? Do you ignore it for a week?

Don amended the sizeable instruction book down to a two-page "Standard" which simply said, "Keep the corners clean" and other similar expectations. In other words, if cockroaches and dust are absent, no need to spend time on the corner.

Another example of standards is when an older teen was trained to clean a building. They showed her the way the rooms were to look. She was given proper equipment and taught skills to complete the job as needed. There was no guesswork and no schedule. It was her call to do everything needed to keep the place looking acceptable.

This approach to cleaning is not abstract — it's an agreed upon set of criterion that both the child and parent understand. Standards are a *condition* of a premise or person; it's not merely checking off 17 repeating items on a daily job list. It's how things should look, not a schedule. With just a bit of standards training and a few basic tools, at the very least kids will have the savvy and ability to keep their personal areas clean. They should also be instructed in what the standards are for the entire rest of the house — otherwise, it's anybody's guess. If mom walks in a room and she goes ballistic, kids know it's probably slipped below her minimal cleanliness standard.

Take time as a family to go on a field trip around the house, room-to-room. Make up and post an agreed-upon list of at least the minimal standards or conditions (how you want it to look) that should be maintained in each area. You might wish to put these in a general order of importance, or maybe feature one room at a time and build on that foundation. Hitting the family with every optimal benchmark at once would be discouraging, so depending on the age and number of your children, rank or divide the standards as you see fit.

Here are some examples of things that could be standards for teen rooms as well as the greater household:

- Clothes: They are either on your body, on a hanger, in the hamper or folded in a drawer or on a shelf.
- Food: Store where intended, toss when outdated. None in the bedroom.
- Beds: Bed is made whenever you are not in it. Bedding is kept sanitary.
- Paper/Mail: Leave nothing unopened; read quickly and file only what you must keep. Toss the rest in the trash.
- Clutter: Don't keep anything that isn't used or enjoyed.
- Study desk: well organized, free of litter and trivia.
- Pictures/Posters: mounted, framed, neatly hung or placed.
- Storage: Most used things should be in prime space; if it's valuable but you don't need it often, box, label and store unobtrusively.
- Trash: Containers clean inside and out, dumped before overflowing
- Dishes: those not in use are put away or stored "dirty" in the dishwasher until run.
- Counter and sink: wiped free of crumbs, spills, build-up and clutter.
- Floors/Carpets: shall be kept free of excessive dust, dirt, spills and clutter.
- Bathroom: Clean, free of soap scum and odors; mirrors and faucets shiny.
- Walls: Shall have no fingerprints, marks, or smudges.
- Furniture: In its place and used for what intended; free of dust and clutter.

> *Danger:* worthless stuff accumulates to the space available. Make a place only for the positive.

- General: cobweb free; dust free, no out-of-season decorations, etc.

After the family collectively decides on what its standards will be for the level of cleanliness you want to maintain, it's up to parents to teach the best techniques for helping kids clean to these standards because there really is no "set" schedule.

Here are some more ideas:

Job Matching. Match jobs to your time, your family's size and age, and abilities.

Team cleaning. Most kids just respond to cleaning better when everybody is a part of the same action. The business world calls it shared governance when the whole is presided over (or in this case, cleaned) by all of its members nearly equally. Natalee makes dinner with mom while Roo sets the table and dad empties out the garbage—all done in the kitchen, at about the same time. Conversation flows, laughter is easy and bonding takes place. After dinner, dad clears the table, Roo unloads the dishwasher, Natalee loads, while mom sweeps the floor. Each project is like a family puzzle, with each person one of the necessary pieces. This system is only

possible if families have some Saturday (or another day) together, or small blocks of evening or early morning hours that are otherwise unscheduled. A further advantage of Team Cleaning is that the children learn a wider variety of jobs. Through example they learn how to do them more correctly, and family cooperation will take off like a rocket. At the very least, one day each month ought to be designated for a "clean the garage" or "plant the garden" or "deep clean the bedroom" project *together*. The house will be more organized, smell and look better, be ready for company at any time, and the kids will learn necessary household skills.

Major Burkepile of the U.S. Marines said of teamwork among his young recruits ages 17 and up, "[They] learn how much easier everything becomes when they put the other guy first and help each other out—whether it's making a rack or cleaning your weapon. When people start helping each other, things get done faster and better." This principle holds true in households as well as on battlefields. Camaraderie grows when we work as a team.

Rooms need to have adequate shelving, drawers that function easily, accessible hampers for dirty clothes, and enough good hangers and space to hang up necessary clean clothing. Hooks, bins and boxes will keep games, accessories and personals divided and organized.

Give 'em what they need. In the movie, "My Big Fat Greek Wedding," every common cleaning problem, as well as just about every other ailment, could be solved by using Windex. How simple that would be! Fortunately, we do need only 3-4 basic chemicals with the right cleaning/applicator cloths to properly care for every household surface—some need to be disinfected, others need to be de-greased, and some have mineral build-up to dissolve away. See www.Live-Right.com.

Regardless of the job to be done, "Now" is the operative word and secret of faster cleaning. You can avoid drudgery later on by cleaning as it becomes necessary.

Work in short spurts. Who wants to clean every Saturday all morning long, or even a solid two hours before bed time? One of the biggest detractors of "doing" is the perceived fatigue factor. And that sets in when we try to do too many of the same things for too long without a break. Even as an adult, I like to work in my home office for two hours max. Then I stand up and wander or pace while making several needed phone calls, or starting dinner, emptying the dishwasher, or doing some laundry. After just 10-minutes, I'm ready to go back to writing again. Kids need the same kind of consideration. Jobs should be carefully assigned, short, and varied. For example, if your teen has five chores that need doing, don't make them all back-to-back cleaning, i.e., doing bathroom mirrors, toilet, counter, floor and bathtub. Consider one wet job, and then assign an additional four others that provide more variation, like sweeping, garbage gathering, clothes folding, or taking a stack of letters to the mailbox. Teens should have the flexibility to do them in any order or sequence, and they can take breaks in between. The secret is to slot cleaning into short spurts now, and avoid the marathon Saturdays later.

> If we give up or compromise in our expectations for young adults responsibility and skill in home environmental care, we are endorsing possible joblessness, marriage failure, poor health, loss of self respect, and rebound families later on.

De-clutter surroundings when kids move out. Kids have a plethora of CDs, DVDs, clothes, make-up, trophies, jewelry, magazines, electronics, shoes, books, socks, underwear, night clothes, hair do-dads, letters, journals, plants, belts, pictures, old school science fair projects, and the list goes on.

Their stuff is their stuff, even if you paid for it. It is futile and improper physically and morally to take complete charge of it; however, if they want to store it at your home after they've moved on, that's another matter. You have every right to assign or limit the space that they continue to occupy—so do it. Don't keep their bedrooms intact, grooming supplies in readiness and kitchen shelves stocked with their favorite flavored yogurt, waiting for their return. Their extra stuff will decrease proportionately to their disappearance if you let it. When kids move out, it's time to S.O.S. (Simplify Our Surroundings).

Work for somebody else. Our older kids want to have money, and they don't necessarily want it all to come from parents. Really! They want the independence of their own money for their own things. It can almost be like having your cake and eating it too for parents if our offspring get jobs where they are paid for learning to work! Think of all the skills related to house and home organization and care that teens can learn right on the job, and get paid while doing it: restaurant hostess, cook and server, cleaning neighbors' homes, being a nanny, working at a dry cleaning store or laundromat, carpet cleaning service, pet watching services and more. These kinds of jobs can sometimes pay a little more than minimum wage (especially with tips), and are widely available to degreeless kids. If their schedule and studies can possibly handle it, encourage them to get a part-time job, just to learn the skills of the trade if nothing more. For some reason (probably known only to psychologists), employers get more mileage out of their young workers through simple expectation than a parent can ever do.

I remember when my youngest daughter got her first serving job at a chain restaurant. My husband and I showed up to order dinner, and watched in amazement as she shuffled between tables, smiling, taking orders, refilling drinks, dropping off bills, serving, and cleaning up. She was a whirlwind of efficiency. At home, it had been a struggle for her to clean off the kitchen counter; here she was whisking away dirty dishes by the dozens. Effortlessly.

Another young man, Taylor Campbell, applied for a general maintenance job at a local swimming resort one summer. When asked if he could clean toilets, vacuum, and pull weeds, he was able to reply with confidence, "Even though I've never been employed by anybody before, I know how to do those things because I do them at home." He got the job.

The quicker our kids get exposed to the real world, the larger their ears and eyes will open to their warehoused parental example and counsel. Jobs for teens and young adults can instill a type of discipline long before final graduations and framed diplomas adorn their walls. Lessons they learn will enrich their lives, create independence, and their standards of order and cleanliness will be raised.

Independent cleaning career. As an independent career, professional cleaning is not a bad consideration. Usually considered low glamour and low pay, it is evolving into a more highly skilled job with opportunities to run small companies and employ people. It is relatively easy to get started in the business and there is minimal financial investment. The world is full of many, many successful people who cleaned their way through school or began successful business careers by cleaning in their teens. Most kids can triple the wage being offered when they independently bid a job (like window cleaning) for someone. This gives them experience in running a small business, balancing a checkbook and being accountable to the government. An excellent book that has launched thousands of young people into successful careers is titled *Cleaning Up for a Living* (Aslett/ Browning, www.Aslett.com). Any resource you can give your child to be self-sustaining is a good move.

Give cleaning gifts. Not the humorous gag gift variety people usually pawn off on our 18-22 year-olds, but truly meaningful, useful items. Think of gifts that assist or encourage cleanliness and order. Cleaning kits, life-time window squeegee sets, shelf organizers, shoe trees, revolving racks, bookcases, display units, bins, boxes and matched baskets. Useful cleaners, tools and organizers will go ten times farther toward the maturation process than comfort foods, more clothes, an updated camera, newer car, overkill tech devices, or cell phone holders ever will. We can't think of a better gift than one of cleanliness and organization — it will teach values forever. Shop at your favorite family store, or visit www. cleanreport.com for reasonably priced, professional quality items. Extension dusters, caddies, the new micro fiber cloths, clever dry erase blocks and no-mess mops are colorful, reasonably priced and really work. A stocked cleaning caddy is every bit as important (if not more so) as their first tool set, hope chest or jewelry box to keep things ready, organized and maintained. Even if their personal cleaning gear amounts to only a few items, they'll take more pride in using it because it's their own. An investment of $20, with a promise of a better household appearance and less sickness (goodbye mold and bacteria) is hard to beat. Plus, it blocks excuses, "*I don't know what to clean with*" and sends a message, "*use me*" by its very presence.

Attend cleaning seminars and workshops. Don is shocked at how many 40-45 year-old women come to him and say how much he influenced their lives for the better, because their mothers drug them to one of his "How to Declutter and Clean" seminars when they were only teenagers. Youth love these completely original events (we call them Cleaning Concerts now!). Because they aren't nearly so set in their ways as we parents, they are much more likely to try what they learn. A really good seminar will teach professional methods that will help them clean whole bathrooms in 3 minutes (kids like speed), melt away mineral build-up safely (it's like a magic show), vacuum properly (they love motors) and mop with ease (they like the water). Time is saved, products are used more correctly and conservatively, and the job is done better.

Use any method you can to get them to a cleaning seminar as young as possible. While there, or next time you're at a professional janitorial supply store or on-line, buy them their own cleaning caddy set (see above). Understanding the dirt and germs theory is possibly more important than learning about birds and bees, if it leads to responsibility and independence.

Whittle **while you work**. Most older teens and young adults want to look desirable and feel good. With the "mating instinct" in the air, more than a few of them think about how they look, night and day. So capitalize on it! Fitness benefits shared at just the right time might be appealing for those trying to lose weight or tone up. If they are counting exact calories, remind them that light cleaning burns about 180 calories per hour; harder jobs like scrubbing floors around 225. Wow! Washing dishes burns three times the calories of sitting in front of the television; and sweeping burns more calories than washing dishes! Vacuuming increases muscle tone and strengthens thighs and calves—this could have great appeal with young women. Guys might go for the yard work and "washing windows builds biceps" angle. Even grocery shopping can be a body building experience when kids simply grasp grocery bags by the handle in each hand, and hold them away from the body while walking from the store to the car. We need to subtly drop these little "fitness opportunity" insights at strategic times and watch them buy in, pitch in, and get in shape!

Clean cupid. Pair up your older teen with a contemporary who is an *Icon of Order* IF you can find one! You can invite the outstanding organizer over for a one-time visit, or hire them. If the friend is close and comfortable with the family, she can be a big help to your daughter with the monstrous task of dejunking and organizing her out-of-control room.

Pair kids off with winners for first-hand peer pressure to put away their blouses, recap their make-up or straighten their shoes. It's right for some kids, IF they agree to it and it doesn't cause them embarrassment. It gets the job done without *you* being the ogre. (It's always easier and more fun to sort through and dejunk the other friend's stuff anyway.)

Shared money. Allowances aren't bad, but performance may run out when the money does; instead, tie the money to household appreciation. To do this, find average costs of electricity, water, gas, travel, and cleaning costs at your house. Figure out what a long shower, over-washed clothes, extra dishwasher loads, lights left on, gas over-used, etc. are. In a family meeting, let all of the kids know what these dollar amounts are, then make this proposal. "If we are all more careful, and help more, we can save some money," you say. "We can reduce our electricity bill by turning off more lights, our gas bill by keeping the heat a little lower, and take shorter showers, etc. Our utilities are $290. If we can get it down to $240 next month, we'd like to split the savings with you!" The kids start to listen at this point. As you hand each of them $10 at the end of the month, even older teens will start thinking twice about carelessly leaving

> Don't let them off the hook—
> if we answer for their personal mess of
> any kind—it's unkind.

the bathroom light on, or taking that eternal shower when no one is around to question them. You get 50% of the savings. This is a low cost, win-win way of teaching responsibility that no university will come up with.

Hate those surprises. Unless it's tied to hard cold cash, a great date, tickets to a concert or game, or perhaps a gift certificate to Nordstrom, don't expect your kids to smile when you throw an idea at them that invades their schedule. They may not already have an actual schedule, mind you, but they don't want one imposed on them on a whim that some cleaning needs to be done right at the moment. We can't stress enough that our young people need to know well in advance what needs to be done around the place. If there's a huge clean-up or organizing project that takes several hours, or even an expectation that the kitchen counter will be cleared, they need to know well ahead!

Set up a family meeting once a month, where standards of household cleanliness are talked about and schedules are set up. Let them know what you want their rooms to look like, and what

the biggie projects are for the month. Get their input on best times to work together on these things. Remind them a week ahead, then a day ahead, and again an hour ahead that things are coming, and they will comply 125% better!

Preparing for the Big One. One of the best ways to get your household in order is to volunteer to have a big event at your home (a reunion, meeting, sleepover, etc.). Raise your hand for the next block party, or offer to have an open house for a friend's wedding. It's a good experience for our young adults to see all that may go into their own future event planning.

Spring cleaning or getting ready to go on a trip might also demand a bit of extra family help, and certainly house selling will require a lot of effort by everyone. Make these monumental moments—the birthday parties,

showers, barbeques, neighborhood parties, reunions, family trips, church parties, and family affairs—times kids will learn not only how to clean before and afterward but feel the energy, experience, and positive outcome of a monumental preparation. They'll be proud of how things look!

Host visitors. Okay, so you don't want the whole ZIP code parading through your front door. You can at least invite a few out of town people to visit. It's exciting when a cousin or a friend from another state or big city comes to town. Besides cleaning preparation, there's some fun nice touches that kids can learn to do which make the experience more pleasant. They can be sure fresh flowers are picked up at the store, or picked from the garden and put into a vase. Little soaps and towels can be set out. A local newspaper is easy to pick up and leave on the pillow. All of these unusual tasks can involve the kids and make them feel like a part of the larger experience. It's not all just about cleaning the shower and toilet, or making sure every cobweb is down, it's about making a "home" a fun place with its own rewards.

The key point. If there is more than one car or one driver in the family, you need to have a common key box at the exit door closest to the cars. If you have no counter space available, you can wall mount small plastic or metal receptacles available at office supply stores very inexpensively. Once people are in the habit of depositing their keys in this box as they enter the house, there will never again be harsh words, frustrating moments and late departures trying to locate car keys. At one point when five of our teenagers were of driving age, we had seven total family cars and seven sets of car keys between us. We all developed such a strong habit of dropping keys in the designated key box (forget hanging them on specific hooks), that I cannot remember even one time where we had to look for any lost keys.

Change is as good as a rest. Just as the "Chance" and "Community Chest" cards are to the game Monopoly, mix in some unusual but doable chores for contrast and novelty. Many of these can be paying jobs for extra money that parents just can't get to, and they are a welcome diversion for the kids. Look around the house for different tasks that are best suited for older teens and young adults—jobs that can also teach them life skills: change air filters, clean air vents, change burned out light bulbs, power wash outside of house, set traps, clean out drains, replace smoke detector batteries, change gaskets, do painting, clean outside windows, trim plants with power hedger, detail the cars and so on. These are finishing touches that convert a minimally functioning household into a place of order and cleanliness.

Provide controls. The epitome of order is to have a *place* for things. Once we know where things are to be kept, there's freedom. It's just like putting the lid back on the lipstick or loose change directly into a coin purse. There is a specified place it's supposed to go! We should do this nearly by habit, because we know where the most convenient, logical home is for each item. Similarly, as older teens prepare to be out on their own, they need to know their place is not the dorm or apartment PLUS their parent's old place. As we mentioned in an earlier section, they are *not* expanding, they are doing a complete shift from address No. 1 to address No. 2. To the extent

possible, recommend that their own new home accommodates 100% of their own stuff. If it doesn't, you'll be a rebound residence forever. It's not helping kids when we encourage or allow dependency by keeping all of their excess stuff (and their bodies) at our place. Turn off your hearing aid to cries and pleas, and give them some personalized labels for their new address. A big garage sale or eBay listing of their discards will yield some bucks to help them on their way. By the time they have completed college or technical training, their former rooms should have been converted into your new office, hobby, exercise or guest room (yes, we want them to occasionally return as guests!).

Conclusion. There are very few kids who seem to be squared away from the birth canal forward—ones whose rooms are an inspirational page from *House Beautiful*. They line up their board games on the left half of shelf No. 1 and their books (in order from smallest to largest) on the right side. Socks are in perfect matched bundles in their designated drawer, and all clothes are hung facing the same direction (with the exact amount of space between each color-coordinated hanger). Trash has recently been emptied, and everything is dusted and perfectly vacuumed. These kids never need to be told to clean their rooms, and they make their beds right as they get out of them. They are natural haters of dirt and disorder. Now I frankly admit that I don't actually know one single kid that does all of these things, but I hear about them from a few bragging moms. My son Ricky stacks his underclothes perfectly on top of each other, folded side outward, and stores them on a certain shelf—just like freshly baked philo dough sections. And he keeps his keys, and loose change corralled in designated separate boxes. That's about as close to a perfect room standard story as I can come up with.

The vast majority of our older kids have all kinds of legitimate (to them) reasons why their own bedrooms, bathrooms, and common areas of the home are of little concern—and certainly not their cleaning responsibility. We threaten and scheme, hoping they will feel some duty, but it's a struggle to get them to comply. Our older children are tougher, smarter and stronger than we give them credit; they have the physical capacity to work hard and not fade. If they know the home improvement task is helping them tone up or lose calories, they may be more inclined to pitch in. If they start to feel a team effort makes their life easier, they will likely participate. Apply these, or one of our many other diplomacies and see some magic things happen. Kids will feel a lot better about themselves if they accomplish something that they can see, and know they have pleased someone. It's OK to ask them to turn off the television or a few of their other electronics. Keep the whole experience light and fun. Our older kids *can* live clean on their own and we can guide them there; cleaning can be a positive!

Section 4: Spouses Cleaning Houses

Man's work and woman's work of past decades was differentiated by outside physical labor and housework. Farm work was typically so brutal that men almost collapsed at the end of the day. They were too far removed from the equally grueling work of the woman who did the cooking, ironing, washing, sewing, and child care, to barely even comprehend it.

Growing up in the 1950's was a relatively simple time for most young families in the United States. Dad went off to work and mom cleaned and managed the home with 2.5 well-fed children pulling at her skirt. There was one car and a single garage to park it in. Few women were in full-time or even part-time careers because dad brought home enough bacon to feed everybody. With economic and attitudinal changes about women's roles, things began to shift decade by decade.

Although most moms now work outside the home for money, they remain largely in charge of how everything functions inside their homes. Women in the 21st Century now *have it all*—all the responsibility of home and family, as well as an expectation to contribute economically.

A Woman's Job to do the Cleaning?

So who says it's the woman's job to clean (and be in charge of everything else home related)? History does. Just

because women joined the workforce, they did not shift out of their home duties. Even the word "shift" is telling. Husbands and fathers worked a day or night shift. When the shift was done, their work was done. Women work three 8-hour shifts at home (even if they aren't present, or are sleeping, they are ultimately in charge), and likely a concurrent "shift" out of the home for a paycheck. Women are expected to keep the house functioning and clean — mostly by themselves. It's almost a universal cry that women want and expect more help from their spouses. (Although there are a small number of households where a role reversal may be in place, we're going to make a wild guess that ninety-three percent of the time it's probably the man who isn't keeping up with his share of the duties.) Today, the blend of skill, knowledge, endurance, and training has blurred gender lines of the past. Most jobs are gender neutral. There is no chore or duty that is able to recognize the size of the hand upon it. Either sex can do the other genders work. Regardless, it is infinitely more difficult to change people's basic natures than the corporate handbook.

As authors and professionals in the field of clean living, we have volumes of books, files, research studies, confessional letters, and papers about spouse (particularly the male variety) cooperation and injustices on the home-front. We've written our own books and have done hundreds of newspaper, radio, and TV interviews on this very subject! Most of the chatter ends up in trivia talk. Few of the solutions from thousands of experts seem to improve the situation much.

Top traditional remedies and strategies seem to be:

1. Divorce the slacker
2. Have compassion and don't expect any help — then you're not disappointed
3. Raise your tolerance level of disorder and dirt
4. Move away from the mess
5. Hire a maid
6. Threaten, nag, or shame them into helping
7. Bribe with money or romantic rewards
8. Hope and pray the mess will be stolen, or go away on its own
9. Go on strike
10. Burn the whole place down

11. Make signs and post honey-do lists everywhere

12. Fake being sick and stay in bed

Most of these solutions aren't solutions at all, just talking points and good fodder for jokes. Because both men and women are now breadwinners, their time at home is limited and the problem of getting things done by fair assignment is dim. There is an additional complication because Generation "X" parents (and even the first of the "Y's") have been used to being "cleaned up after" themselves,

> Most men would rather change a diaper than scrub a bathroom. Scrubbing bathrooms is on "the bottom of the task hierarchy."
> –Julie E Brines, sociologist at the University of Washington

which worsens the problem. Added to that, we have created an excessively busy social structure of too much stuff, bigger homes, more gadgets and gizmos, loads of comfort products, extreme child demands, high debt factor, and, to be sure, more creative excuses for not cleaning from both genders.

We sense spoken and unspoken dialog similar to this:

1. I had a really hard week at work – (And you assume I didn't?)

2. I didn't get a degree in plastics manufacturing to do the dishes – (So, did you invent a no-wash dish while you were getting that degree?)

3. You're better at it – (So you obviously need the extra practice, not me!)

4. I wouldn't know where to start – (A simple "yes" would be wonderful.)

5. I'd just botch it up if I did it anyway – (Anyone who messes up should be smart enough to clean up.)

6. It's my day off — (Tell the diapers that.)

Is it true that men just don't have an aptitude for cleaning? Consider the fact that men own 70% of all the U.S. professional cleaning companies! And more than 50% of their employees are also men. Hmmm. Gotta make you wonder what happens to their cleaning capabilities when they step over the threshold of their own homes. Are they grime blind? *Miami Herald* humor columnist Dave Barry quipped that "Women, for hormonal reasons, can see individual dirt molecules, whereas men tend to not notice them until they join together into clumps large enough to support commercial agriculture." More accurately, I think some men develop a sudden selective blindness. For these few, all but the television screen is obscured to view, making them not too much more useful than exotic household pets.

"How do spouses divide up the housework? One of my neighbors works upstairs and her spouse works downstairs. Another lady had hip surgery and finally got her husband to help with the housework. But it took a major thing to get him to help."
—Janet T.

Avoid the old yours and mine. There is yet another percentage of the male gender who is self-righteously helpful. How do you feel when the macho man of the house says, "Dear, tonight I'm going to do *your* dishes," then "vacuum *your* floor" and "fold *your* laundry." And we reply, "Wow! Is this my birthday or something?" Excuse me, since when do *moms* have ownership of all the goods and jobs in the home? Do we own the appliances, dishes, towels and clothing that need upkeep? It would be proper to respond to this spouse, "You mean, you'll help with *the* dishes? Why, thank you, dear." This is one of several methods to encourage spousal support—and for the right reasons. Here are a few more suggestions that may work for you.

Divide errand running. One super-demanding practice in a mutual relationship is when one spouse deems the other their slave. Sub-consciously they inflict a constant "help me honey" or "fetch" imposition on each other. We've all heard these indirect subtleties:

"While you're up, I wouldn't mind another glass of water."

"I think I will have a piece of pie now."

"Have you seen my shoes?"

"Where are you hiding the scissors these days?"

"It's time to feed Fifi."

"How about another refill on the lemonade?"

"I'm starving. What is there to eat?"

"Looks like the fire is going out…"

"We're out of toilet paper in here!"

If you find yourself blurting out any of these presumptuous phrases to your mate, at least offset with some accolades. Responding to needs voluntarily is the highest form of giving, but don't just assume you should be waited on. Run your own errands more and "volunteer" to run each other's—it's magic to the relationship!

By the way… Roses and anniversary rings are great surprises! So are show tickets, cute outfits, and homemade pie. You can just spring them on your spouse and be assured of getting only a positive response;

however, when you get a cleaning brainstorm idea, people need to mentally and physically adjust. If your mate comes home after work, or has a Saturday free and is making or has big personal plans and you spring a "We've got to do," or "Would you do?" job on them, suddenly cooperation becomes shaky. There are very few emergencies (except for spills) that ought to appear in cleaning, clutter or organizational plans. "Awareness" generates more willingness than an "ambush."

Along with squelching job surprises, we recommend that neither spouse add more work onto the original task. We have a tendency, when we get the momentum going, to add on more than we set our time and commitment to do: "Honey while you're at it would you mind doing this, and this, and this, and maybe this too?" A rare emergency "to do" is okay when done with some kindness, but not when it's a trick played on a captive audience.

Junk knows no gender. Without a doubt, the single biggest challenge to keeping a home is clutter control. Clutter adds time to any project. Before you will ever be successful keeping a home looking good, you need to separate yourself from the contents of your house. Yes, even in the closest marriage one person's junk can be the other's irritation. So first agree that the unused gadgets, outdated medicines, and leftover fabric, etc, have to go. Next, use friendly persuasion as you sort through stuff which may be junk to you but is gold to them. If you can clutter clean together, that will be a foundation of an ongoing bonding activity. It's kind of like trimming up trees or bushes. It's a pain to do it, but it sure looks better when it's done. So make the effort to get rid of the excess around you that's insulating you from each other and causing stress between you and your partner.

We are all accomplished junkers, and our personal stuff likely takes up much more than its share of the bedroom. We clean over, under, and around all of our excess. We have stuff stashed away that we can't remember, is outdated, and that we'll never use again. You would cringe if you knew how many couples have called or written to us about their spouse's junk… "Every note he ever took in medical school, three classic cars (none of which run), twenty-five years' worth of *Modern Photography*, his great-grandfathers lawn bowling trophies, a guitar with no strings, an expensive (and ugly) collector's decanter, luckless lottery tickets, dusty and dismembered radios and TVs, the high school yearbooks we haven't looked at since we graduated, the stamp collection he was very hot on in the fifth grade, the wreckage of his model of the *Santa Maria*, elaborate equipment for a succession of hobbies like fly tying and bowling (which he's lost interest in or never gotten around to doing), and at least a half-pound of official-looking unidentified keys are among our closest roommates now."

Work together to clean everything

out, and don't worry if one of you happens to be the bigger junker—we all think that about each other. Be kind, and be decisive, but work together to clean out your clutter.

The best way to get each other to toss the goods is by example. "Hey look, Melissa, my dusty tackle drawer is all dejunked and organized!" Jump up and click your heels—and watch him attack his old cassette tapes next.

When you've gotten through your personal closets, drawers, den, glove compartment, and that cave of clutter known as the garage, you can move on.

Throw out the trash and give the usable stuff to the charity of your choice. If you can't bear to part with something, put it in an "Emotional Withdrawal" box and seal it. Three months later, if you haven't had to open it back up, you can chuck the box (you won't remember what's in there, so it won't hurt a bit). Dejunking can also be privately done, and it will be liberating, and fun! Side note: Just remember, probably 40% of cleaning time, cost and unwelcome emotion come from excess. So unstuffocate away!

Don't be ashamed. Having established our position on clutter, do remember that all around us is proof of our existence. There needs to be a balance of human occupation with clutter occupation. We don't need or want museum homes. We live in our homes and shouldn't pretend otherwise. I remember as a young child, our insurance guy came to the door and we had a sewing mess all over the living room carpet. I apologized profusely, and excused the mess, even at age 10. I was conditioned to do so. He then complimented my mom on my manners—and my behavior was reinforced. As I look back on that moment in my life, that material laid out all over the living room floor was productive and beautiful—it was pure evidence that home sewn Easter dresses for young daughters, were on their way.

Our houses are to function for us, not grace the pages of *House Beautiful* (which I think is well named; it's not a home beautiful, it's a house beautiful). *Better Homes and Gardens* still isn't real (it should be Bigger Homes and Gardens). Bottom line, you need to strike a balance between just letting the house happen to you and perfection (only 1 in 55 homemakers is immaculate).

And a little breathing room.
Even after your household cleaning policies or *standards* are written up (see previous chapters), and everything is decluttered to the extent that you are comfortable, and chores are being performed without hassle, allow some wiggle room. If we're too fussy (it's only done right if it's as good as mom does it), we'll shoot ourselves in one of our own two tired feet. We've got to let all of the household helpers know that their efforts are not only appreciated, but adequate. If it's truly a blundered job, work *with* your spouse next time until they get up to speed.

Ask before outlining. I know "close" companions shouldn't have to ask each other (or plead and beg) for help. Idealistically we should sense it, but in a crowded, survival-mode schedule, expectation is buried in busyness. Sincere ignorance is a reality. We are each often blind to another's needs or have grown so familiar with a glaring need that it is overlooked. Sharing (making public) our goals, wants, and wishes ahead of time, makes a mate aware, and more inclined to do it instead of being ordered or assigned. People work better when

they volunteer for a task. Sadly, we often end up leaving sarcastic notes or posted orders in an attempt to solicit help. For decades this husband/wife communication has been referred to as the "Honey Do" list; the man is the honey, the woman is the executive issuer. Maybe we should change the word "Honey" to household? The better approach is, "This needs to be done, honey, how shall *we* do it?" It's easier on the ego to choose rather than to be assigned. People like to please much more and more often than hurt or disappoint.

This is the Place. If our homes are cluttered and disorganized, spouses may really, truly not know where to put things, even if they had a burning desire to help. Not knowing where certain things go is a big hindrance to the desire to help clean and organize. So make sure it's easy to see where to put the TV trays, toy groups, tablecloths and so on. Have a rack or other clearly designed area for reading materials and wastebaskets in plain sight. Even if wives plan the menu, and do the bulk of the grocery shopping, men should be able to unload and know where every single item goes—from mayonnaise to macaroni, and from toothpaste to toilet paper. If they claim cluelessness, show them, item by item, where to put everything; but don't give in and do it all yourself.

Surrender, just a little.

"Always do the dishes right after dinner!"

"Sheets must be changed twice a week. That's how my mom did it."

"I don't want to discuss anything until the garbage is taken out."

"Did you really trim these rose bushes, or just wound them a little?"

"You call that clean?"

"That has to be done over again."

There's a time to let some things wash. Leaving a germ or streak, forgetting one wastebasket, mismatching socks, leaving the toilet

seat up, a temporarily lost hammer or a pair of scissors isn't worth a fight or even a threat. We all can nit-pick even the best quality work. If we settle for a 75% made bed or 60% clean shower, it is better than letting them go entirely untouched. We call small imperfections on a construction completion job a "punch" list. That's literally what it ends up being at home when we corner or contest with each other over a minor quality shortfall—especially on the first stumble with an unfamiliar task in another's charted territory. Demanding perfection from yourself is a personal call, but demanding it out of another is "home-a-cide!" We often assign work and then insist on a result beyond perfection. No one is inspired by that. Let a sleeping dog lay (and dust around him). Aggressively redoing a half-done task brings pure alienation from our spouse. Hide the grimace and give a sincere "not bad!" approval. It might encourage another shot at it.

A third party's opportunity.
There is some point at which household necessities (previously done 100% by either spouse) are just not worth the time or effort anymore. Some women have wisely (and economically) figured

out a great solution to the dreaded surprise guest dinner: OUTSOURCE! Some men have finally realized laundries can clean their long-sleeved dress shirts fast, well, and cheap, and give the former in-house laundry maid relief to do some more personal and important things instead. Professionals can present a welcome and effective resource for lots of house care. Maids are moral. Even though Don owns a landscape business, all his lawn and flowers at his business are contracted out to others. Remember, only a few years ago we did all of our own hair cuts, tire changing, car servicing, painting, canning, carpet cleaning, moving, and sewing. Many of those tasks are now wisely outsourced. A good question to ask is, "Should we hire someone to do it?" and "Can we afford it?" That way there is no whining when the bill comes, and more appreciation when the job is done.

The hunting game. We learned years ago that extra effort usually dissolves ambition. If any of us has

> A Study by M.D. Manufacturing found that 81% of men report more frequent vacuuming by themselves if they have a central vacuum in the home

to drive or walk too far, or wait too long, we're inclined to give up on the idea. Just not knowing where a needed item is when you are ready for it dampens your diligence. Hunting for an extension cord, a hammer, a key, a cloth, or a vacuum when you are fired up to do a task will cool down your enthusiasm by 43 degrees. If it doesn't turn up fast you will "turn off," as well as adopt a suspicious mistrust for a next time you try. So if you want to get your spouse involved in cleaning you need to make it easier to find things needed for the project and easier to put away all that stuff around the home.

Our society has made order and organization complicated. There are hundreds of time management seminars going on each day, but still most of us never feel in full control of our time or our homes. If the contents and necessities of the home each had their place and these items were returned where they have immediate access—cleanliness would improve. In the kid's chapter, we referred to this as having an "address" for everything. Think of all the conflict, blaming, and negative environment instantly created when either spouse or child begins hunting for something that is not in its place. Intensity of irritation increases with the diminishing hope of successful location. And how many cop-outs come from, "I would if I could find the ___ ___ (matches, Band-aids, cell phone, pencil, etc.)."

CIA: Convenience, Immediacy and Abundance. From Don's 50 years experience in the domestic cleaning industry he's made a profound observation. We don't have days, or even hours, set aside to clean. It is generally minutes, and too often we spend five minutes rounding up the gear to do one minute of cleaning.

What we need is supplies that are CIA (convenient, immediate, and abundant), then the chance that either the kids or spouse will actually do it is enormously enhanced. Make a special effort to have a designated caddy, cart or shelf with fresh, organized, and ready cleaning supplies and tools.

Any object (machine/mechanism) that doesn't work well discourages the use and user. Things that clean and maintain are generally on the low end of the list of purchases or improvements. The No. 1 ragtag tools of the house are most often the cleaning related items from the washing machine to rusty wire storage racks. This projects an unimportant aura around our efforts to clean. The really sad surprise to this unfortunate

condition is that more money and more time are used to buy junk juices (chemicals) and cheap brushes and mops than it would have cost to buy the very best up front. The best often takes up less room and is much more effective and easy to use. Many grocery store tip books and popular magazine articles steer homeowners to traditional home remedies (baking soda, bleach, vinegar, powdered cleanser and toothbrush mentality), all of which are relatively ineffective for fast, dynamic cleaning. The successful solution we simply counsel is to use and do what the pros tell us. They have squeezed cleaning to a science of safety, quality and economy, and today there is little difference between commercial and domestic surfaces and their cleaning needs. Can't find what you need? We have resources that the old janitor and scrubwomen of yesterday didn't have—the Internet, for starters. In a few minutes of searching (without driving across town), you can locate a menu of the cleaners, machines, and even instructions that the pros use at janitorial companies. Many items are obtainable through mail order, shipping for much cheaper than the cost of your

time and gas to pick up an inferior product at the grocery store. You will notice a marked difference in your spouse's attitude and how much more quickly they complete a cleaning job when using products that work.

Efficient carriers. Cleaning gear usually gets tossed under the sink or randomly hung or propped in some nearby closet. With a tiny bit of effort and money, commercial caddies can be filled with needed supplies for that job or area, and can be stored neatly under the sink, on a shelf or suspended on a wall. There's less damage to surface areas because the caddy controls spills and ring burns. Face it, we are a drive-in, grab-and-go society at home as much as on the road. This leaves no lost time and no excuse for being clueless as to the whereabouts of the needed items. There are great new family-friendly household sized cleaning carts! They fit in a closet or small corner, and hold everything you need. The carts travel along with you to all areas of the house. It's like a mobile cleaning closet on wheels! (see www.Live-Right.com).

A factor called "When." Before we get into the best time to do things, clouded by "he's always an early riser," and "she's such a night person" labels, we need to look at *what* there is to do. Dishes, laundry, clutter, and papers accumulate during the day. Bulking accumulated duties into one big day to do one big cleaning will result in the fastest disintegration of home care togetherness imaginable for five reasons:

1. It takes a big block of time: homecare is sellable in minutes, avoided in hours.

2. The accumulative visual mess that constantly haunts the whole family is like noticing flies on the apple pie you plan to eat later. Yuck. Avoidance.

3. We often pick Saturday or Sunday to "do the job," and this clearly cheats us out of a "want to do" day. Still, an occasional half day on Saturday can be a positive.

4. Regardless of your religious beliefs, doing maintenance work on Sunday is bad timing. That's not the day to wake up and start the week by cleaning. In our current society we are expert players, and anything that interrupts our golf to go-karts play day feeds negative vibes.

5. Nor is night a good time to wash the car or collect the trash, etc. When it's late, everybody is tired and often on edge.

The time most conducive to mutual (husband/wife) or entire family help is a combination of morning and NOW! Morning offers objective discipline. Generally everyone is home and everyone has energy. The old on-the-run, too-busy, we're-gonna-be-late mornings (for school, jobs, etc.) need an earlier discipline.

In one minute right NOW, each of us can quickly hand clean or load the dirty dishes. In 5 seconds we can put away the salt and pepper, or screw on the loose lid and totally eliminate a heap of work later; in fact, anything left undone will only get harder to deal with later. Wet and soft hot cake dribble can be wiped up in 5-seconds! Let it set until Saturday's big cleanup time and it's 5-minutes of scrubbing time, with scraping tools and dissolver

> Praise works best with spouses; money works best with teens; and playtime best with young kids for rewards.

chemicals. Clothes have to hang up sometime. Now, instead of later, creates an encouraging all-day inspiration.

Selectivity is for little kids. When full grown adults proudly stick out their chest and say, "I don't do windows," we ask them, "Well, who does?" Favorite jobs are for five-year-olds. Fathers, mothers, and teens need to memorize the axiom: "life isn't always doing what you like, it's liking what has to be done." A little trading is OK but overall your hands and heart can and should fit any requirement. Eliminate the old, immature, "I don't like to…," "I would rather…," "Why me?" "I just hate to do…" "If you think I'm going to do that…" Just doing the job that needs to be done, gives a confidence that overcomes the thoughts of displeasure. Amazingly, most un-favorites become favorites. And mates, just like kids, never reach a time when they don't want to be appreciated after facing a new challenge, so be sure to congratulate and commend your loved one after they've done one of these needed deeds.

Freedom of choice. Here is capitalizing on America's freedom of choice at its finest.

Prepare a "Stand Around List." We all have personal "to do" lists, so what about the house having one of its own? The couple makes it up together. It's a list which, regardless of what, when, and how can be tackled by anyone. It is a no-surprise outline that offers cause and direction, and thus subdues irritants. Write down every change that you would like to see your home have. Put them in order of time, cost, aesthetics, or technology headings. The jobs then become a home improvement checklist, not a honey do list to make the husband feel guilty.

Signs posted here and there. A few signs around can also work to encourage some action. Since men aren't impressed, and are probably overwhelmed with so many jobs in a vertical row, break up your wishes and post them where needed. A small note by the stack of newspapers in the corner might read, "please take us to recycling." Next time your spouse lifts up the toilet lid, there could be a love note on the underside, "please take three minutes and clean me." Not only will you get a smile after looking at the sign (for several days), you might just get some action!

Come right out and ask for help if necessary. And be specific! Our spouses are distracted, tired, and unaware—just like we are. Maybe some just need to be jolted into action. For example, after a meal simply say, "Who'd like to rinse? Load? Wipe the table? I'll clear up the leftovers and put them into the fridge." After all, everyone seems to cheerfully, dutifully clear their own table at McDonald's! Why? Because it's expected. Most people love to help, they just need to be directed. In your very strongest good-natured way, express some real thanks when they help out. The more sincere you are, the more likely they are to do it again, or to do more than asked.

What to do for date night? Since there are few decent movies, and ice cream means an extra two miles of walking just to burn off the extra calories, try a different kind of date night. Occasionally there will be an area seminar on how to clean, how to dejunk, or how to organize. Keep your eyes on newspaper listings, university-based forums, or check www.napo.com (National Association of Professional Organizers) for local events. These classes are entertaining and may well

be just the incentive your loved one needs to get the mop moving. Someone said, "While I truly love your hugs and kisses, what I love most is help with the dishes." If food is the way to a man's heart, maybe used mop water is the way to a woman's?

Worth the effort? Try reward of multiplication. At a cleaning seminar a few years ago, a woman picked up a copy of a cleaning book, walked up to Don's wife and asked earnestly, "If I buy this will it really help my husband clean?" Don's wife opened the book, pointed to some of the most popular parts, and said, "Mrs. Walker, there are over 100 short lessons for your husband in this book, and encouragements to start helping with the household chores. But if he reads the whole thing and only does one single job, even a little thing like turn his socks or underwear right side out before tossing them in the laundry basket…if he learns or does only that one thing from the whole book, and does it the rest of his life, that's at least 10,000 times that you won't have to do it for him!" (Mrs. Walker bought six books; one for each of her sons-in-law.)

Just ask people (nicely) to

straighten and clean their own mess, instead of moaning and groaning and muttering incomprehensible phrases at them. Taking a little time to raise awareness or change a habit can mean a lifetime of not having to pick up or hang up behind yourself or a careless clutterer.

A final word. The overall answer to consistent help is not found on the lists, in bribes, from seminars, through guilt infusing or through begging. The answer has been around forever but is seldom recognized. It's explained in a short word that glorifies helping. The all-solving, all-healing, motivating word is GIVE. Post the word and live it.

To give is the ultimate expression of love. Mankind instinctively yearns to *give* his/her all to whomever or whatever they love and respect—be it a person, project, or property. There exists no measurement or tracking in

sincere giving. When it happens, it strengthens relationships. People that respect and appreciate who they have and what they have don't really need to be told, assigned, begged or threatened to produce.

If we really love somebody as much as we love ourselves, we'll give.

But behind the good intention to give there are some basic "genetic" factors:
1. Men like (love) to please women
2. Women respond to being pleased

Reverse that? It still works for a great relationship. I think men are not as sharp or wise as to what pleases women the most. Tradition has it that flowers and candy are the ultimate charmers, followed by a sprinkle of jewelry, perfume, dinner, and a closet with some new seasonal outfits hanging inside. All of these are appreciated on occasion, but you can't place any

> "Love between spouses generates a desire to help; sharing comes naturally because there is mutual consideration. Once my parents were retired dad began doing more of the household chores. They have evenly divided task lists that they do every week. Basically, my parents share all the responsibilities of their home because they desire to build an eternal relationship built on love and consideration."
>
> —Lynn Wright

of them on even the same page as the benefit of consistent *giving* in the care of home and family!

Cleaning for 15 minutes or 5 hours is not the issue. It's caring enough to do what is needed. It doesn't matter who did it last time either. All that counts is that we each do what needs doing, so we can enjoy a clean, neat, setting. So jump in and give. And don't keep score!

Bionic Spouses

BIONIC stands for "Believe It Or Not I Care." Let's be bionic spouses!

Conclusion

You deserve a break today every day!

Each spring we get calls to participate in interviews and media events associated with spring cleaning! Our interviewers expect to hear hints and tips that rely on using vinegar, baking soda, toothpaste, hairspray, mayonnaise and home-based remedies. Quick fixes stay popular with major magazines, and on radio and television, because old wives tales have audience charm. Ironically, most of them don't work at all.

We never fall prey to using or recommending gimmicks when solid solutions are available—and neither should you. The answer to cleaner and better functioning homes will not found in bottles of lemon juice, peanut butter or Tang. The real answer is discovered when we 1) design cleaning out of our homes and 2) inspire teens, kids and spouses to participate and do their part.

Household efficiency. Household efficiency made possible through *house design* and trained *helping hands* isn't just possible for the family down the street! They may be tuned into a few more resources than you, or seem to have the right system or method in place, but *you* can have a home that rivals the best. In fact, it can function optimally and set the standard for the neighborhood!

Design or build it out? You've thought about the possibility hundreds of times! We suspect some of your own ideas are even better than the few we spring-boarded here to get you thinking (Section One). If you use the "design it out" approach, it will reduce house care up to 40% instantaneously! Even one or two minor changes will deliver results for as long as you live in the house. While most people *think* about this option, very few get serious enough to actually incorporate it in their structural or final finishes. Don't let tradition, habit, doing it like the contractor advises or like your mother-in-law threatens, deter you. If you want a break from a big share of cleaning tasks—be bold and creative and design your house to do some of the work.

If you gleaned only two ideas from INSPIRING KIDS TO CLEAN (Section Two), we hope they are: "Don't give up—and don't give in!" This determination will put you ahead of 50% of parents struggling to cement the cleaning doctrine into their child's life. If you apply an additional solution or two, keep with it. Every successful concept you teach them will ignite another and another. Your kids are just as clever as anybody else's, and they can do their part extraordinarily well—so let them.

As for our TEEN CLEAN MACHINES and young adults (Section Three), you may think your kids are hopeless, but any trade with those of a similar age from another family would be a wash. Stick with them until they strike out on their own. They learn best when you lean on them a bit because they are not completely sold on the importance of clean. With love and a whole lot of patience, they'll come through and make you proud.

The conversion to SPOUSES CLEANING HOUSES may be a slow one (Section Four). You might see just 10% results in the first year, but then it will jump up to 30%, and even 50% (by the time you are grandparents!). But that's improvement, and however slow or meager, it's help you would not have had otherwise. The concept is not only exciting but entirely possible. You have read several fresh approaches to help you each eliminate some of the ever present clutter-causing disagreements, work at house projects together, and even try out a creative date at a cleaning concert. Don't let them pass you by.

We build houses for show, for shelter, and as an investment. But we can also build *sharing* homes, ones that share the workload, as they connect family members to each other. Through solutions targeted to keep order at home, time-saving designs and methods will save you a lot of regret and stress. And for sure you will easily recognize and ignore all the shallow hints and tips out there that really don't work!

Make the break—a Clean Break!

—Sandra Phillips
Don Aslett

What concept in the book helped you most?

Please share your story! Do you have favorite ways to make your home easier to keep clean? Are there more ideas for getting kids, teens or to spouses help?

Send us your comments at www.Live-Right.com or via email at: sandraphillips@live-right.com

References

Defining Clean

Clean (Klen)
Adj. clean•er, clean•est
  Free from dirt, stain or impurities; unsoiled.
  Free from foreign matter or pollution; unadulterated: clean air

Phrasal Verbs:

Clean Out
1. To rid of dirt, rubbish, or impurities
2. To empty of contents or occupants

Clean Up
1. To make clean or orderly
2. To make oneself clean, neat, or presentable
3. To dispose of

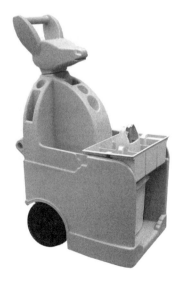

Klean-GuRoo™ Cleaning Cart

This world famous cleaning cart is like having a cleaning closet on wheels. Light and maneuverable, Klean-GuRoo moves effortlessly around the house with you saving you time and energy by conveniently organizing more than 30 basic cleaning products and tools. Take Klean-GuRoo to the source of the mess rather than hauling your supplies all over your home, office, motorhome, or wherever, and have your entire arsenal ready to go at a moments notice. Easy to use and kids love it. It will revolutionize the way you clean! Available from Live-Right products.

Little Joey Cleaning Caddy:

The Little Joey Cleaning Caddy is a convenient and versatile 6-compartment caddy designed with ease of use in mind. With its ergonomic handle the Little Joey makes it easy to quickly transport your most commonly used cleaning products saving you time and effort. The Little Joey features four extra-deep corner pockets to prevent spilling and plenty of room on board for wet or dry cloths and sponges, it's your one-stop cleaning shop! Available from Live-Right products.

Basic Cleaning Kits:

A simple cleaning kit should contain: professional spray bottles filled with all-purpose cleaners, glass cleaner, heavy duty cleaner, terry cleaning cloths, dusters, white scrub sponge, and Micro fiber cloths. For bathrooms, add disinfectant cleaner, shower cleaner, grout brush, bowl cleaner, toilet swab, pumice stone and rubber gloves. Along with anything else you need for common problems in your home.

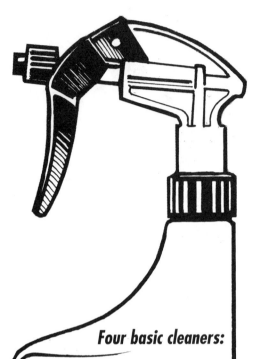

Four basic cleaners:

Neutral All-Purpose. Neither acid nor alkaline, so it's safe for almost any surface. A mild but effective general cleaner for most everyday use.
Heavy-Duty Cleaner/Degreaser. A high pH cleaner with strong dirt-dissolving action for the tough and greasy jobs.
Glass Cleaner. A fast-evaporating alcohol-based cleaner for when you need a streak-free shine on windows, mirrors, chrome, appliance fronts and fixtures.
Disinfectant Cleaner. For areas and surfaces that need sanitizing, like bathroom, sickroom, garbage cans, etc.

We'd love to hear from you!

Tell us about your cleaning challenges and successes!

Speaking - Seminars - Consulting
Live-Right
PO Box 1185

Whittier, CA 90609-1185

www.live-right.com
SandraPhillips@Live-Right.com

To order products online
visit www.live-right.com
or call 1-800-451-2402

Mon. thru Fri. 7:30a - 6p MST

We are committed to enriching lives by creating
order and promoting harmony.